ALL OF MY VIOLET EGODDESSES ARE MY WIVES

KEITH N. FERREIRA

iUNIVERSE, INC.
BLOOMINGTON

All of My Violet eGoddesses Are My Wives

iUniverse books may be ordered through booksellers or by contacting:

iUniverse
1663 Liberty Drive
Bloomington, IN 47403
www.iuniverse.com
1-800-Authors (1-800-288-4677)

ISBN: 978-1-4502-9214-6 (sc)
ISBN: 978-1-4502-9215-3 (ebk)

Printed in the United States of America

iUniverse rev. date: 02/03/2011

Books by Keith N. Ferreira

The Intellectual Rebel
Aphorisms
Speculative Aphorisms
Speculative Aphorisms II
Philoscience
Philoscience II
Intellectual Jazz
Intellectual Jazz II
Jazzism
Neoliberal Arts
Neoliberal Arts II
Postmodern Minimalist Philosophy
Simpletism
Uncertaintyism
The Ultimate Truth
Anything Is Possible
Political and Social Observations
The University of Neoliberal Arts
A New Breed of Philosophers
Ferreirism - The Ultimate Philosophy
The eChurch of Zerotropy
The Ferreira Genesis Equation
Zerotropism and Panaceanism

Philosophy Should Belong to the Masses
Programming the World with Philosophy
The Masses Should Think for Themselves
The Masses Educated Can Never Be Defeated

Please visit my website at: *http://www.philophysics.com*

Thank You!

All of My Violet eGoddesses Are My Wives (Part One)

All of my Violet eGoddesses are my wives. So says, Dr. Keith N. Ferreira. Thus speaks, Dr. Victor Frankenstein II of the Pilot Pen. Believe it or not! May the Source be with you! QED! (9/29/10)

The Earth is now obsolete, and irrelevant. So says, Dr. Keith N. Ferreira. Thus speaks, Dr. Victor Frankenstein II of the Pilot Pen. Believe it or not! May the Source be with you! QED! (9/29/10)

Earth is about looks, and now everything on Earth looks shitty. So says, Dr. Keith N. Ferreira. Thus speaks, Dr. Victor Frankenstein II of the Pilot Pen. Believe it or not! May the Source be with you! QED! (9/29/10)

Earth is about looks, and now everything on Earth looks shitty. So says, Dr. Keith N. Ferreira. Thus speaks, Dr. Victor Frankenstein II of the Pilot Pen. Believe it or not! May the Source be with you! QED! (9/29/10)

There is no way in hell blacks and Jews can ever catch up, and overtake my Violet eGoddesses. So says, Dr. Keith N. Ferreira. Thus speaks, Dr. Victor Frankenstein II of the Pilot Pen. Believe it or not! May the Source be with you! QED! (9/29/10)

Eating of the fruits of the Tree of Knowledge for free can also be a death sentence! Every fool knows that! Do you out there in the world know that as well! So says, Dr. Keith N. Ferreira. Thus speaks, Dr. Victor Frankenstein II of the Pilot Pen. Believe it or not! May the Source be with you! QED! (9/30/10)

I guess that I am also a High-Tech Voodoo Knowledge Tree. So says, Dr. Keith N. Ferreira of the Pilot Pen. Believe it or not! May the Source be with you! QED! (9/30/10)

All the Laws of Nature from the human perspective are still guesses, conjectures, assumptions, and hypotheses, because exact quantifiability, and measurability prove nothing in the long run! So says, Dr. Keith N. Ferreira of the Pilot Pen. Believe it or not! May the Source be with you! QED! (9/30/10)

Let us make the assumption (hypothesis) that philosophy is dead! Now, what follows from such an assumption??? Does that mean that one should abandon philosophy?? Does that mean that we should end the world? So asks, Dr. Keith N. Ferreira of the Pilot Pen. Believe it or not! May the Source be with you! QED! (9/30/10)

I am more valuable than all the expert advisors in the world, today: Individually and collectively! So says, Dr. Keith N. Ferreira of the Pilot Pen. Believe it or not! May the Source be with you! QED! (9/30/10)

Drummond North is code for: Drum on North Stars. And, Polly Drummond is code for: Many drum ons, which is code for many pariahs. And, pariahs are code for outcasts in Hindustani, in Hindustan, which is in Northern India. Pariahs are calm musicians who make music for a living. So says, Dr. Keith N. Ferreira of the Pilot Pen. Believe it or not! May the Source be with you! QED! (9/30/10)

Eating of the fruits of the Tree of Knowledge for free can also be a death sentence! Every fool knows that! Do you out there in the world know that as well! So says, Dr. Keith N. Ferreira. Thus speaks, Dr. Victor Frankenstein II of the Pilot Pen. Believe it or not! May the Source be with you! QED! (9/30/10)

I guess that I am also a High-Tech Voodoo Knowledge Tree. So says, Dr. Keith N. Ferreira of the Pilot Pen. Believe it or not! May the Source be with you! QED! (9/30/10)

All the Laws of Nature from the human perspective are still guesses, conjectures, assumptions, and hypotheses, because quantifiability, and measurability prove nothing in the long run! So says, Dr. Keith N. Ferreira of the Pilot Pen. Believe it or not! May the Source be with you! QED! (9/30/10)

Let us make the assumption (hypothesis) that philosophy is dead! Now, what follows from such an assumption??? Does that mean that one should abandon philosophy?? Does that mean that we should end the world? So asks, Dr. Keith N. Ferreira of the Pilot Pen. Believe it or not! May the Source be with you! QED! (9/30/10)

I am more valuable than all the expert advisors in the world, today: Individually and collectively! So says, Dr. Keith N. Ferreira of the Pilot Pen. Believe it or not! May the Source be with you! QED! (9/30/10)

Drummond North is code for: Drum on North Stars. And, Polly Drummond is code for: Many drum ons, which is code for many pariahs. And, pariahs are code for outcasts in Hindustani, in Hindustan, which is in Northern India. Pariahs are calm musicians who make music for a living. So says, Dr. Keith N. Ferreira of the Pilot Pen. Believe it or not! May the Source be with you! QED! (9/30/10)

I would like blacks and Jews to watch the Movie: Planet of the Apes (1969). Is that what you really wanted? http://www.imdb.com/video/screenplay/vi3430940953/ (9/28/10)

I would like blacks and Jews to watch the Movie: Planet of the Apes (2001). Is that what you really wanted? http://www.imdb.com/video/screenplay/vi3481272601/ (9/28/10)

The World Automatic Moral Discipline Exchange is now up an running! So says, Dr. Keith N. Ferreira of the Pilot Pen. Believe it or not! May the Source be with you! QED! (9/30/10)

The Violet eGoddesses Automatic Moral Discipline Exchange is now up an running! So says, Dr. Keith N. Ferreira of the Pilot Pen. Believe it or not! May the Source be with you! QED! (9/30/10)

The UFOs Automatic Moral Discipline Exchange is now up an running! So says, Dr. Keith N. Ferreira of the Pilot Pen. Believe it or not! May the Source be with you! QED! (9/30/10)

The All of Creation Automatic Moral Discipline Exchange is now up an running! So says, Dr. Keith N. Ferreira of the Pilot Pen. Believe it or not! May the Source be with you! QED! (9/30/10)

The UFOs that have been protecting the world from destruction for more than fifty years, now, are my UFOs. So says, Dr. Keith N. Ferreira of the Pilot Pen. Believe it or not! May the Source be with you! QED! (9/30/10)

The solution to what is happening in the the world today is Poker and false pockets. So says, Dr. Keith N. Ferreira of the Pilot Pen. Believe it or not! May the Source be with you! QED! (9/30/10)

The UFOs that have been protecting the world from destruction for more than fifty years, now, are my UFOs. So says, Dr. Keith N. Ferreira of the Pilot Pen. Believe it or not! May the Source be with you! QED! (9/30/10)

Haloperidol is code for: Halo Perimenter High-Tech Voodoo Doll! So says, Dr. Keith N. Ferreira of the Pilot Pen. Believe it or not! May the Source be with you! QED! (9/30/10)

In the Roman Catholic Tradition: Both Monks and Nuns are Married to Jesus Christ: Their savior! So says, Dr. Keith N. Ferreira of the Pilot Pen. Believe it or not! May the Source be with you! QED! (9/30/10)

What are the motives of the people behind those who create video games of any kind? So asks, Dr. Keith N. Ferreira of the Pilot Pen. Believe it or not! May the Source be with you! QED! (9/30/10)

Superconductors are conductors that conduct electricity without resistance. In other words, superconductors are linear circuits, because they cannot do otherwise, but tow the line, due to the fact that they have no resistance, or cannot resist the flow of electricity. So says, Dr. Keith N. Ferreira of the Pilot Pen. Believe it or not! May the Source be with you! QED! (10/1/10)

What happened to the so-called "scapegoat" that was released into the wild a long time ago? So asks, Dr. Keith N. Ferreira of the Pilot Pen. Believe it or not! May the Source be with you! QED! (10/1/10)

America makes scapegoats (those who are forced to be homeless, etc.) of its best and brightests, because America is wild about religion. So says, Dr. Keith N. Ferreira of the Pilot Pen. Believe it or not! May the Source be with you! QED! (10/1/10)

What happened to the so-called "scapegoat" that was released into the wild a long time ago? So asks, Dr. Keith N. Ferreira of the Pilot Pen. Believe it or not! May the Source be with you! QED! (10/1/10)

America makes scapegoats (those who are forced to be homeless, etc.) of its best and brightests, because America is wild about religion. So says, Dr. Keith N. Ferreira of the Pilot Pen. Believe it or not! May the Source be with you! QED! (10/1/10)

Telescopes and opera glasses were probably invented in countries that had harems, among the rich and wealthy. So says, Dr. Keith N. Ferreira of the Pilot Pen. Believe it or not! May the Source be with you! QED! (10/1/10)

Is the world still convinced that we are not in cyberspace? So asks, Dr. Keith N. Ferreira of the Pilot Pen. Believe it or not! May the Source be with you! QED! (10/1/10)

Most arguments that are won by debates show no signs of creativity, whatsoever! Therefore, debates are not the most superior form of creative activity known to humanity, because most debates show no signs of creativity, whatsoever! So says, Dr. Keith N. Ferreira of the Pilot Pen. Believe it or not! May the Source be with you! QED! (10/1/10)

Why are all Roman Catholic countries poor, and unfree? So asks, Dr. Keith N. Ferreira of the Pilot Pen. Believe it or not! May the Source be with you! QED! (10/1/10)

Let me state again that there is an infinite number of unique and useful creative ideas (concepts) still waiting to be discovered in all realms of learning! In other words, academia is a hotbed of creativity! And, if you really believe that, then you are really dumb! So says, Dr. Keith N. Ferreira of the Pilot Pen. Believe it or not! May the Source be with you! QED! (10/1/10)

Haiti is code for: The Hate Key!, which is code for: The Key to Hate! So says, Dr. Keith N. Ferreira of the Pilot Pen. Believe it or not! May the Source be with you! QED! (10/1/10)

I have got a family to feed, too: All nonblack peoples of the world! So says, Dr. Keith N. Ferreira of the Pilot Pen. Believe it or not! May the Source be with you! QED! (10/1/10)

I hope that the world thinks that I am a good Shoemaker!, and a good Carpenter!, and a good Gardener!, and a good Bullshitter!, Etc., etc., etc. So says, Dr. Keith N. Ferreira of the Pilot Pen. Believe it or not! May the Source be with you! QED! (10/1/10)

The Frothmeter Test is a very inexpensive and accurate means of testing all kinds of original and creative ideas (concepts) out to determine the validity of mindblowing and revolutionary new ideas (concepts)! Just visit the appropriate college or university department, and tell the secretary in charge that you would like to speak to the appropriate professor about an idea (concept) that you want to test out on the professor. When the professor reads your idea (concept), please check for the quantity of froth that is coming out of the professors mouth! The greater the amount of the froth coming from the professors mouth, the greater the probability that your idea (concept) is correct! Especially, if the idea (concept) is mindblowing and revolutionary! The Frothmeter Test is a very serious, and accurate test for mindblowing and revolutionary new ideas (concepts). So says, Dr. Keith N. Ferreira of the Pilot Pen. Believe it or not! May the Source be with you! QED! (10/1/10)

Student organizations should consider getting copyrights, trademarks, and patents, etc., for their members! And, the student organizations should get a cut of any royalties that accrue from marketable copyrights, trademarks, and patents, etc.! So says, Dr. Keith N. Ferreira of the Pilot Pen. Believe it or not! May the Source be with you! QED! (10/1/10)

Academia is now irrelevant to (for) the progress (advancement) of knowledge and wisdom! So says, Dr. Keith N. Ferreira of the Pilot Pen. Believe it or not! May the Source be with you! QED! (10/1/10)

The answer to the question: Who betrayed America? Is: The American Teachers. About five years ago, I saw video footage of American teachers, who came back from China jumping for joy at the sight of Chinese children who were merely camouflage, for a national effort to educate all the genius children in China, which totalled between one hundred and three hundred million Chinese children! The video footage showed Chinese children answering rapidly any question that was asked of them!, and the American teachers fell for such a stupid ass trick. So says, Dr. Keith N. Ferreira of the Pilot Pen. Believe it or not! May the Source be with you! QED! (10/1/10)

The Human Brain Intranet is now up and running in the brains of the genius children of the world! In other words, the different faculties (mathematics, science, literature, etc., etc., etc.) of their brains are now intracommunicating with each other! Therefore, it would be interesting to check the brainwave patterns (electroencephalographs) of their brains to see if their brainwave patterns are different from ordinary (average) children. The Chinese scientists said that the genius children with integrated brains have different brainwave patterns than ordinary (average) children. So says, Dr. Keith N. Ferreira of the Pilot Pen. Believe it or not! May the Source be with you! QED! (10/2/10)

Please check to see if all children can benefit from the Human Brain Intranet Phenomenon, because it might benefit most of the children of the world. So says, Dr. Keith N. Ferreira of the Pilot Pen. Believe it or not! May the Source be with you! QED! (10/2/10)

The teachers (Shamans, witch doctors, modern teachers, etc.) were struggling like crazy for the last ten thousand years or so to prevent the Human Brain Intranet Phenomenon from occurring in the children of the world, and, consequently, the adults of the world, as well! Therefore, modern teachers, parents, etc., must have known instinctively about the Human Brain Intranet Phenomenon, and they were "are" instinctively opposed to the Human Brain Intranet Phenomenon. And, that is what the struggle in education for the last ten thousand years or so was, and still is about!: Postmodern Minimalist Philosophy, aka Neoliberal Arts. So says, Dr. Keith N. Ferreira of the Pilot Pen. Believe it or not! May the Source be with you! QED! (10/2/10)

The modern struggle in education is about the Human Brain Intranet Phenomenon (HBIP), and its pros and cons. And, the struggle is far from over, worldwide! And, that is what the World Grassroots Democratic Revolution (WGDR) is really all about!: Postmodern Minimalist Philosophy, aka Neoliberal Arts! So says, Dr. Keith N. Ferreira of the Pilot Pen. Believe it or not! May the Source be with you! QED! (10/2/10)

I believe that children of multi-ethnic backgrounds should be given an escape hatch to educate themselves, especially, if they do not identify with any one ethnic group! For instance, I identify with all ethnic groups of the world, but I do not identify with any one ethnic group! So says, Dr. Keith N. Ferreira of the Pilot Pen. Believe it or not! May the Source be with you! QED! (10/2/10)

Why do blacks, especially, find it incumbent upon themselves to oppose me, and my philosophy, especially, with such toxic venom. So says, Dr. Keith N. Ferreira of the Pilot Pen. Believe it or not! May the Source be with you! QED! (10/2/10)

The dumbass Christians in my neighborhood, probably do not even know that they are living in a Ghetto community, that is analogous to the Ghetto community in "The Merchant of Venice" by William Shakespeare. http://en.wikipedia.org/wiki/The_Merchant_of_Venice So says, Dr. Keith N. Ferreira of the Pilot Pen. Believe it or not! May the Source be with you! QED! (10/2/10)

Instinctively, all babies know about the dangers, and tragedies that are associated with circumcision! And, that is the main reason why all babies cry like hell before they are circumcised! So says, Dr. Keith N. Ferreira of the Pilot Pen. Believe it or not! May the Source be with you! QED! (10/2/10)

Circumcision (both male and female), produces such symptoms as: The death wish for all life; Psychological linear circuitry (Towing the line), etc., etc., etc. In other words, circumcision is not a harmless operation, because it produces all kinds of bad biochemistry in the human body and mind! So says, Dr. Keith N. Ferreira of the Pilot Pen. Believe it or not! May the Source be with you! QED! (10/2/10)

Circumcision (both male and female), produces such symptoms as: The death wish for all life; Psychological linear circuitry (Towing the line), etc., etc., etc. In other words, circumcision is not a harmless operation, because it produces all kinds of bad biochemistry in the human body and mind!: http://en.wikipedia.org/wiki/Foreskin_ restoration Personally speaking, I do not think that the biochemistry associated with pre-circumcision, or non-circumcision can be restored by current methods of foreskin restoration. So says, Dr. Keith N. Ferreira of the Pilot Pen. Believe it or not! May the Source be with you! QED! (10/2/10)

There are probably powerful hormonal glands in the foreskin of both non-circumcised males and females that cannot be restored by current methods of foreskin restoration to circumcised human males and females. However, the powerful hormones from the hormonal glands can be isolated and synthesized, artificially, and prescribed for circumcised males and females. So says, Dr. Keith N. Ferreira of the Pilot Pen. Believe it or not! May the Source be with you! QED! (10/2/10)

The educational struggle is the focal point (key) to all other human struggles! So says, Dr. Keith N. Ferreira of the Pilot Pen. Believe it or not! May the Source be with you! QED! (10/2/10)

The educational struggle in the last ten thousand years of so, has been the struggle to prevent students, and thus adults from integrating the various faculties, such as language, logic, and mathematics, etc., of their brains into the Human Brain Intranet (HBI). So says, Dr. Keith N. Ferreira of the Pilot Pen. Believe it or not! May the Source be with you! QED! (10/2/10)

Anabolic enzymes might be the key to the creation of life on Earth! And, they might also be the key to the evolution of life on Earth! So says, Dr. Keith N. Ferreira of the Pilot Pen. Believe it or not! May the Source be with you! QED! (10/2/10)

The powerful trace chemicals and/or biochemicals in the foreskin glands of human beings, might be trace amounts of powerful catabolic/anabolic enzymes that catalyze/anabolyze chemicals/biochemicals such as DNA molecules, etc. directly in the bloodstream, which then end up in the brain and/or other organs of the human body! So says, Dr. Keith N. Ferreira of the Pilot Pen. Believe it or not! May the Source be with you! QED! (10/2/10)

The powerful trace chemicals and/or biochemicals in the foreskins of both non-circumcised males and females might not be restorable by current methods of foreskin restoration. However, those powerful trace chemicals and/or biochemicals in the foreskins of both non-circumcised males and females can be isolated and synthesized, artificially, and prescribed for circumcised males and females. So says, Dr. Keith N. Ferreira of the Pilot Pen. Believe it or not! May the Source be with you! QED! (10/2/10)

Most people believe that life isn't fair, and they are satisfied with the status quo, or even worst! So says, Dr. Keith N. Ferreira of the Pilot Pen. Believe it or not! May the Source be with you! QED! (10/2/10)

I want all the peoples of the world to focus, especially on the kids of the world: The younger the better! So says, Dr. Keith N. Ferreira of the Pilot Pen. Believe it or not! May the Source be with you! QED! (10/2/10)

In America, especially, philosophy websites are very dangerous! So, if you smarty pants, and smarty panties out there want to stay alive, especially in America, please stick with my websites, especially! So says, Dr. Keith N. Ferreira of the Pilot Pen. Believe it or not! May the Source be with you! QED! (10/2/10)

It is the parents who prevent babies from speaking too early. For the above reason, most babies have many nervous breakdowns before they are allowed to speak (vocalize). Babies recover rapidly from nervous breakdowns, due to the lack of opportunities to vacalize, but they do have many nervous breakdowns, that are caused by their parents preventing them from speaking too early. So says, Dr. Keith N. Ferreira of the Pilot Pen. Believe it or not! May the Source be with you! QED! (10/2/10)

I came to America in order to have a Global reach for my ideas. So says, Dr. Keith N. Ferreira of the Pilot Pen. Believe it or not! May the Source be with you! QED! (10/2/10)

I came to America in order to have a Global reach for my ideas. So says, Dr. Keith N. Ferreira of the Pilot Pen. Believe it or not! May the Source be with you! QED! (10/2/10)

My Violet eGoddesses can multiply their numbers in an instant. That just goes to show how powerful they are. In other words, my Violet eGoddesses are all over the universe and beyond. So says, Dr. Keith N. Ferreira of the Pilot Pen. Believe it or not! May the Source be with you! QED! (10/2/10)

If the governments of the world have problems that they cannot solve, they should not hesitate to consult the babies of the world, because they might be surprised to find out that the babies of the world have already got the answers. So says, Dr. Keith N. Ferreira of the Pilot Pen. Believe it or not! May the Source be with you! QED! (10/2/10)

Russia does not want to play third, forth, or fifth fiddle anymore to the West, when it can now play first fiddle on the world stage. I warned the EU years ago that this could happen, but now it is too late in the international political game! Now most of the developing countries of the world are out-maneuvering the USA, in deal making, etc., on the international stage. So says, Dr. Keith N. Ferreira of the Pilot Pen. Believe it or not! May the Source be with you! QED! (10/2/10)

I suspect that the cosmic rays focusing lenses in Italy are very huge, and inexpensive, when compared to modern day high-energy particle accelerators. Italy got the idea for the huge cosmic rays focusing lenses from me over the Old Telepathic Internet decades ago! The Italian physicists said that they used dirt clays as lenses to focus the cosmic rays onto ordinary detectors. So says, Dr. Keith N. Ferreira of the Pilot Pen. Believe it or not! May the Source be with you! QED! (10/2/10)

To me, my skin is not worth not doing philosophy, especially Postmodern Minimalist Philosophy, aka Neoliberal Arts. Also, no amount of human, or divine deaths, including my own death, can dissuade me from doing philosophy, especially Postmodern Minimalist Philosophy, aka Neoliberal Arts. So says, Dr. Keith N. Ferreira of the Pilot Pen. Believe it or not! May the Source be with you! QED! (10/2/10)

My mathematics, especially, is more powerful than any God(s) or Goddess(es) in all of Creation. So says, Dr. Keith N. Ferreira of the Pilot Pen. Believe it or not! May the Source be with you! QED! (10/2/10)

Americans are mental microbes. So says, Dr. Keith N. Ferreira of the Pilot Pen. Believe it or not! May the Source be with you! QED! (10/2/10)

Putin (Put in) Pirate Parties Around the World!: http://en.wikipedia.org/wiki/Pirate_Parties_International So says, Dr. Keith N. Ferreira of the Pilot Pen. Believe it or not! May the Source be with you! QED! (10/2/10)

My next door neighbor, Mr Todd the Part-time Rabbi, told me over the New Telepathic Internet that I am the Top Rabbi in the world, although I am not even a Jew! So says, Dr. Keith N. Ferreira of the Pilot Pen. Believe it or not! May the Source be with you! QED! (10/2/10)

I know that my mathematics consists of discoveries that I made about Nature! I never said that I created (invented) my mathematics! So says, Dr. Keith N. Ferreira of the Pilot Pen. Believe it or not! May the Source be with you! QED! (10/3/10)

It had to be MI5 (The British Foreign Intelligence Service) that said, "Catch as catch can!," because all I said was, I am the minutest particle! Catch me, if you can! If you catch me, I will disappear, and run away! Catch me, if you can! The Americans weren't that sophisticated, then! And, they are still not that sophiscated, now! Logic is logic! And, that is that! I did all this at the tender age of about five or six years old! So says, Dr. Keith N. Ferreira of the Pilot Pen. Believe it or not! May the Source be with you! QED! (10/3/10)

I do not wish to be a part of anybody's club (Inner circle). So says, Dr. Keith N. Ferreira of the Pilot Pen. Believe it or not! May the Source be with you! QED! (10/3/10)

Clubs (Inner Circles) are analogous to primitive multicellular living organisms! So, why should I want to join the Inner Circles of a club? In other words, clubs (Inner Circles) have the mental capacities of primitive multicellular living organisms. For instance, most (Inner Circles) do not believe in God, or the Bible, yet they all want to fulfill the prophecies of the Bible. So says, Dr. Keith N. Ferreira of the Pilot Pen. Believe it or not! May the Source be with you! QED! (10/3/10)

The Italian physicists said that they have got about one hundred huge (enormous) cosmic rays lenses for carrying out high energy cosmic rays detectable collisions, which are detectable with ordinary detectors, all over Italy, because the lenses are scalable! So says, Dr. Keith N. Ferreira of the Pilot Pen. Believe it or not! May the Source be with you! QED! (10/3/10)

The Americans said that they are not interested in smart people anymore! So, the EU should kick the USA out of CERN, NATO, and Europe! So says, Dr. Keith N. Ferreira of the Pilot Pen. Believe it or not! May the Source be with you! QED! (10/3/10)

The Italians say that my new concept for cosmic rays lense arrays for carrying out high energy cosmic rays detectable collisions is an excellent idea! This new idea could drop (cut) the cost of huge (enormous) cosmic rays lenses for high energy cosmic rays detectable collisions from 50 million dollars each to 25 million dollars each. So says, Dr. Keith N. Ferreira of the Pilot Pen. Believe it or not! May the Source be with you! QED! (10/3/10)

The world has to reeducate America, because America has lost its way! But, America, probably will not listen, because Americans are now very arrogant! Believe it or not! May the Source be with you! QED! (10/3/10)

For very creative people, forgetting/recalling is very important. In other words, forgetting/recalling is extremely important for creative minds! For example, in the expression: The absent-minded professor! I guess it is all stardom (stardumb) professors, now! So says, Dr. Keith N. Ferreira of the Pilot Pen. Believe it or not! May the Source be with you! QED! (10/3/10)

It is not necessary to know a lot, in order to do a lot, creatively, because all that is necessary, in order to do a lot, creatively is to know the basics of a lot of academic, and nonacademic disciplines. I am living proof that with just basic knowledge, and an integrated brain, children can do incredibly fantastic, creative, and original stuff! So says, Dr. Keith N. Ferreira of the Pilot Pen. Believe it or not! May the Source be with you! QED! (10/3/10)

My Special Theory of Relativity proves that we are living in cyberspace. And, it indirectly proves that all spaces are cyberspaces. So says, Dr. Keith N. Ferreira of the Pilot Pen. Believe it or not! May the Source be with you! QED! (10/3/10)

If the world were to forget about Sir Isaac Newton, the world will be as good as dead! So says, Dr. Keith N. Ferreira of the Pilot Pen. Believe it or not! May the Source be with you! QED! (10/3/10)

The almost certainty that all spaces are cyberspaces opens up such possibilities that anything in Nature is possible for real. So says, Dr. Keith N. Ferreira of the Pilot Pen. Believe it or not! May the Source be with you! QED! (10/4/10)

If human fetuses are supercomputers, then what about the fishes, etc. So says, Dr. Keith N. Ferreira of the Pilot Pen. Believe it or not! May the Source be with you! QED! (10/4/10)

The almost certainty that all spaces are cyberspaces opens up such possibilities that anything in Nature is possible for real. Such are the possibilities of the Ferreira Theory of Cyberspaces. So says, Dr. Keith N. Ferreira of the Pilot Pen. Believe it or not! May the Source be with you! QED! (10/4/10)

I hope that I have convinced that world that Ulti Ne Plus Ultra is a dumbass idea. In other words, Ulti Ne Plus Ultra = Plus Ultra, for real! So says, Dr. Keith N. Ferreira of the Pilot Pen. Believe it or not! May the Source be with you! QED! (10/4/10)

The almost certainty that all spaces are cyberspaces opens up such possibilities that anything in Nature is possible for real. So says, Dr. Keith N. Ferreira of the Pilot Pen. Believe it or not! May the Source be with you! QED! (10/4/10)

If human fetuses are supercomputers, then what about the fishes, etc.? So asks, Dr. Keith N. Ferreira of the Pilot Pen. Believe it or not! May the Source be with you! QED! (10/4/10)

The almost certainty that all spaces are cyberspaces opens up such possibilities that anything in Nature is possible for real. Such are the possibilities of the Ferreira Theory of Cyberspaces. So says, Dr. Keith N. Ferreira of the Pilot Pen. Believe it or not! May the Source be with you! QED! (10/4/10)

I hope that I have convinced that world that Ulti Ne Plus Ultra is a dumbass idea. In other words, Ulti Ne Plus Ultra = Plus Ultra, for real! So says, Dr. Keith N. Ferreira of the Pilot Pen. Believe it or not! May the Source be with you! QED! (10/4/10)

If humanity wants to understand why, Ulti Ne Plus Ultra = Plus Ultra, then they should contemplate the number line, where any contiguous section of the number line has an infinite number of mathematical points! Therefore, (Ulti Ne Plus Ultra = Plus Ultra) = The Law of Uncertaintyism!, which brings us back to Socrates': "I know that I know nothing!" In other words, I surrender to the ancient Greek philosophers, philosophically speaking! So says, Dr. Keith N. Ferreira of the Pilot Pen. Believe it or not! May the Source be with you! QED! (10/4/10)

My Violet eGoddesses know everything, already! So, I guess that we have now arrived at the bottom of the rabbit hole! So says, Dr. Keith N. Ferreira of the Pilot Pen. Believe it or not! May the Source be with you! QED! (10/4/10)

Humanity, etc., have to entertain my Violet eGoddesses, because otherwise, my Violet eGoddesses would be bored (board) stiff. In other words, philosophy, etc., are not at an end for human beings. So says, Dr. Keith N. Ferreira of the Pilot Pen. Believe it or not! May the Source be with you! QED! (10/4/10)

The evidence is mounting everyday that we are, indeed, living in cyberspace! In other words, the evidence is overwhelming that we are, indeed, living in cyberspace. So says, Dr. Keith N. Ferreira of the Pilot Pen. Believe it or not! May the Source be with you! QED! (10/4/10)

All measurements of relative time, in Einstein's Special Theory of Relativity, involve gravity/acceleration. Therefore, I remain convinced that $T = T(\text{sub } 0)$ for relative velocity in the Ferreira Special Theory of Relativity. So says, Dr. Keith N. Ferreira of the Pilot Pen. Believe it or not! May the Source be with you! QED! (10/4/10)

In 1972, US government scientists told me not to wait for them, because they will just slow me down. So, I am telling the world community, who can understand my mathematics, etc., not to wait for the West to catch up with you, because they will just slow you down, and keep you back. Therefore, go ahead and not wait for the West to catch up with you! So says, Dr. Keith N. Ferreira of the Pilot Pen. Believe it or not! May the Source be with you! QED! (10/4/10)

A worrier is a warrior, and vice versa! So Says, Dr. Keith N. Ferreira. Thus speaks, Dr. Victor Frankenstein II of the Pilot Pen. Believe it or not! May the Source be with you! QED! (10/5/10)

My Violet eGoddesses know everything already for real! So Says, Dr. Keith N. Ferreira. Thus speaks, Dr. Victor Frankenstein II of the Pilot Pen. Believe it or not! May the Source be with you! QED! (10/5/10)

Worriers are warriors, and vice versa! So Says, Dr. Keith N. Ferreira. Thus speaks, Dr. Victor Frankenstein II of the Pilot Pen. Believe it or not! May the Source be with you! QED! (10/5/10)

Tradition is a common excuse for not thinking for oneself! In other words, if one is not thinking for oneself, then one has to be ritualizing. So says, Dr. Keith N. Ferreira of the Pilot Pen. Believe it or not! May the Source be with you! QED! (10/4/10)

Zero over slash counter slash = Z, where Z is the mark of Zorro, and Zorro stands for zero entropy, according to the Neolaw of Entropy, by Dr. Keith N. Ferreira of the Pilot Pen. So says, Dr. Keith N. Ferreira of the Pilot Pen. Believe it or not! May the Source be with you! QED! (10/5/10)

Cactus can be code for: Dr. Keith N. Ferreira cacked the US, which can be code for: Dr. Keith N. Ferreira fucked the USA!!! So says, Dr. Keith N. Ferreira of the Pilot Pen. Believe it or not! May the Source be with you! QED! (10/5/10)

Circumcision causes pseudo-rabies in human beings. So says, Dr. Keith N. Ferreira of the Pilot Pen. Believe it or not! May the Source be with you! QED! (10/5/10)

ALL OF MY VIOLET EGODDESSES ARE MY WIVES (PART TWO)

Circumcision causes pseudo-rabies in human beings. So says, Dr. Keith N. Ferreira of the Pilot Pen. Believe it or not! May the Source be with you! QED! (10/5/10)

Christians are pseudo-rabid dogs. So says, Dr. Keith N. Ferreira of the Pilot Pen. Believe it or not! May the Source be with you! QED! (10/5/10)

I am also King David II: King of Israel, and all the Jews of the world. So says, Dr. Keith N. Ferreira of the Pilot Pen. Believe it or not! May the Source be with you! QED! (10/5/10)

If I am a schemer, then the Jews are schematics! In other words, a schemer is one who designs schematics! So says, Dr. Keith N. Ferreira of the Pilot Pen. Believe it or not! May the Source be with you! QED! (10/5/10)

Jerusalem can be code for: Jews rule all of them: From Greater Newark, Delaware, USA. The City of Jerusalem is not important. But, what is important is the concept that encompasses the name Jerusalem. So says, Dr. Keith N. Ferreira of the Pilot Pen. Believe it or not! May the Source be with you! QED! (10/5/10)

I am a good bullshitter, and that means that I am a good fuckshitter! So says, Dr. Keith N. Ferreira of the Pilot Pen. Believe it or not! May the Source be with you! QED! (10/5/10)

I am a great bullshitter, and that means that I am a great fuckshitter! So says, Dr. Keith N. Ferreira of the Pilot Pen. Believe it or not! May the Source be with you! QED! (10/5/10)

I am Leona Helmsley II, and I say that all the rituals in the world belong to the little people of the world. So says, Dr. Keith N. Ferreira of the Pilot Pen. Believe it or not! May the Source be with you! QED! (10/5/10)

Students of all ages should organize in order to get their ideas (concepts) copyrighted, patented, and trademarked, etc., and they can all share in the benefits of having their ideas (concepts) copyrighted, patented, and trademarked, etc. So says, Dr. Keith N. Ferreira of the Pilot Pen. Believe it or not! May the Source be with you! QED! (10/5/10)

I am an intellectual plantation owner, and I am planting Tea (Truth) seedlings into the ground all over the world, so that the Tea (Truth) trees might grow into intellectual Tea (Truth) trees, because I am an intellectual Tea (Truth) farmer from Trinidad & Tobago, in the Caribbean Sea (See). So says, Dr. Keith N. Ferreira of the Pilot Pen. Believe it or not! May the Source be with you! QED! (10/7/10)

"Now I am become Death, the destroyer of worlds!:" This quote was taken from the Upanishads of India, by J. Robert Oppenheimer (April 22, 1904 - February 18, 1967). So says, Dr. Keith N. Ferreira of the Pilot Pen. Believe it or not! May the Source be with you! QED! (10/5/10)

I am an intellectual plantation owner, and I am planting Tea (Truth) seedlings into the ground all over the world, so that the Tea (Truth) trees might grow into intellectual Tea (Truth) trees, because I am an intellectual Tea (Truth) farmer from Trinidad & Tobago, in the Caribbean Sea (See). So says, Dr. Keith N. Ferreira of the Pilot Pen. Believe it or not! May the Source be with you! QED! (10/7/10)

Medicine, education, religion, etc., have always been weapons of war: Both psychological and nonpsychological. So says, Dr. Keith N. Ferreira of the Pilot Pen. Believe it or not! May the Source be with you! QED! (10/7/10)

The Ark of the Covenant is older than Judaism by an infinite number of years! It appears to me that the Ark of the Covenant contained a type ancient advanced technology that was UFO based. http://www.jewishvirtuallibrary.org/jsource/Judaism/ark.html So says, Dr. Keith N. Ferreira of the Pilot Pen. Believe it or not! May the Source be with you! QED! (10/7/10)

I was preparing for my life of knowledge and adventure, before I was even born! So says, Dr. Keith N. Ferreira of the Pilot Pen. Believe it or not! May the Source be with you! QED! (10/7/10)

In Nazi Germany, there were pariahs beating drums, also!: A mouth, or a pen, etc., can also be a drum! So says, Dr. Keith N. Ferreira of the Pilot Pen. Believe it or not! May the Source be with you! QED! (10/7/10)

He cactus more than once. In fact, he cactus so many times that he doesn't even remember how many times that he cactus. So, says Leona Helmsley II! Thus speaks, Dr. Keith N. Ferreira of the Pilot Pen. Believe it or not! May the Source be with you! QED! (10/7/10)

The psychotherapeutics of postmodern minimalist philosophy, aka Neoliberal Arts, is infinitely superior to Jewish psychotherapy. So, says Leona Helmsley II! Thus speaks, Dr. Keith N. Ferreira of the Pilot Pen. Believe it or not! May the Source be with you! QED! (10/7/10)

Enzyme is code for: End zee people of the Limestone Cliffs of Dover! So, says Leona Helmsley II! Thus speaks, Dr. Keith N. Ferreira of the Pilot Pen. Believe it or not! May the Source be with you! QED! (10/7/10)

Leona Helmsley II is his Queen of Mean! So, says Leona Helmsley II! Thus speaks, Dr. Keith N. Ferreira of the Pilot Pen. Believe it or not! May the Source be with you! QED! (10/7/10)

If the Turds, the Nerds, and the Geeks were to master my websites, then they will be able to go on and conquer the world, and the solar system, for now! So, says Leona Helmsley II! Thus speaks, Dr. Keith N. Ferreira of the Pilot Pen. Believe it or not! May the Source be with you! QED! (10/7/10)

The Internet, and the World Wide Web are not controlled from the USA, and they haven't been controlled from the USA for about ten years now. So, says Leona Helmsley II! Thus speaks, Dr. Keith N. Ferreira of the Pilot Pen. Believe it or not! May the Source be with you! QED! (10/7/10)

Foreign countries can see inside of America without cameras, period. And, this technology is decades old. So, says Leona Helmsley II! Thus speaks, Dr. Keith N. Ferreira of the Pilot Pen. Believe it or not! May the Source be with you! QED! (10/7/10)

Science lost, religion lost, and Art won (One)!: Our Father who Art in Heaven, period!: Postmodern minimalist philosophy, aka Neoliberal Arts! So, says Leona Helmsley II! Thus speaks, Dr. Keith N. Ferreira of the Pilot Pen. Believe it or not! May the Source be with you! QED! (10/7/10)

Ambrosia (Postmodern minimalist philosophy, aka Neoliberal Arts), which is the food of the Gods, is infinitely more pleasurable, and rewarding than gambling, sex, or drugs. So, says Leona Helmsley II! Thus speaks, Dr. Keith N. Ferreira of the Pilot Pen. Believe it or not! May the Source be with you! QED! (10/8/10)

How can children think for themselves, if teachers want to keep forcing them into intellectual, scientific, and cultural molds? So, says Leona Helmsley II! Thus speaks, Dr. Keith N. Ferreira of the Pilot Pen. Believe it or not! May the Source be with you! QED! (10/8/10)

Name a William Shakespeare that Teachers created! So, says Leona Helmsley II! Thus speaks, Dr. Keith N. Ferreira of the Pilot Pen. Believe it or not! May the Source be with you! QED! (10/8/10)

Teachers have never created anything of any important caliber whatsoever! So, says Leona Helmsley II! Thus speaks, Dr. Keith N. Ferreira of the Pilot Pen. Believe it or not! May the Source be with you! QED! (10/8/10)

It is a myth that black people are religious, or spiritual! Thus, working from such foundations, one can go on to prove that all peoples are God killers! So, says Leona Helmsley II! Thus speaks, Dr. Keith N. Ferreira of the Pilot Pen. Believe it or not! May the Source be with you! QED! (10/8/10)

Teachers cannot mold or shape creativity, because molding or shaping creativity is an oxymoron! In other words, creativity can only be molded or shaped internally, because creativity is personal. And, that is why the best teachers volunteer no information, in the classroom. So, says Leona Helmsley II! Thus speaks, Dr. Keith N. Ferreira of the Pilot Pen. Believe it or not! May the Source be with you! QED! (10/8/10)

Teachers cannot mold, or shape creativity, because molding or shaping creativity is an oxymoron! In other words, one does not mold, or shape creativity, because creativity "flows like [Turbulent] water" to use a phrase that Bruce Lee used, so famously. So, says Leona Helmsley II! Thus speaks, Dr. Keith N. Ferreira of the Pilot Pen. Believe it or not! May the Source be with you! QED! (10/8/10)

Immortal Technique: What you are engaging in is a form of philosophy: You fucking asshole! I am the fucking Government http://www.youtube.com/watch?v=j7Vl0peys90 So, says Leona Helmsley II! Thus speaks, Dr. Keith N. Ferreira of the Pilot Pen. Believe it or not! May the Source be with you! QED! (10/8/10)

Everyone wants something for nothing, which will never happen in this universe! Go and educate yourselves! God will provide! So, says Leona Helmsley II! Thus speaks, Dr. Keith N. Ferreira of the Pilot Pen. Believe it or not! May the Source be with you! QED! (10/8/10)

Everyone in the world has a record, period, down to the minutest details, in my files computers, which are scattered all over the universe and beyond! So, says Leona Helmsley II! Thus speaks, Dr. Keith N. Ferreira of the Pilot Pen. Believe it or not! May the Source be with you! QED! (10/8/10)

One does not need a personal guru anymore, unless one wants to be exploited! Please use the Internet, and the World Wide Web (WWW) for all your research needs. Tell all the gurus in the world to go and fuck themselves. So, says Leona Helmsley II! Thus speaks, Dr. Keith N. Ferreira of the Pilot Pen. Believe it or not! May the Source be with you! QED! (10/8/10)

Everyone is wearing a mask, and beneath the mask, is another masks, etc., etc., etc., to infinity. So, says Leona Helmsley II! Thus speaks, Dr. Keith N. Ferreira of the Pilot Pen. Believe it or not! May the Source be with you! QED! (10/8/10)

Anyone who believes that the world should be bombed back to the twelft century, or even futher back is a Jackass (Jack ass). So, says Leona Helmsley II! Thus speaks, Dr. Keith N. Ferreira of the Pilot Pen. Believe it or not! May the Source be with you! QED! (10/8/10)

All surfaces [sur (Sir) faces] are faces! And, surface can be code for: Absurd faces! So, says Leona Helmsley II! Thus speaks, Dr. Keith N. Ferreira of the Pilot Pen. Believe it or not! May the Source be with you! QED! (10/8/10)

A schemer is one who designs schematics!: http://en.wikipedia.org/wiki/Circuit_diagram So, says Leona Helmsley II! Thus speaks, Dr. Keith N. Ferreira of the Pilot Pen. Believe it or not! May the Source be with you! QED! (10/8/10)

Molehills can exist anywhere on great mountains, because moles are parasites! So, says Leona Helmsley II! Thus speaks, Dr. Keith N. Ferreira of the Pilot Pen. Believe it or not! May the Source be with you! QED! (10/8/10)

If the world can see, hear, etc., inside of America without cameras, microphones, etc., then imagine how these types of technologies can be, and are being used in science, technology, spying, etc.! These types of technologies are more than forty years old. And, I am responsible for these types of technologies, etc., and more! So, says Leona Helmsley II! Thus speaks, Dr. Keith N. Ferreira of the Pilot Pen. Believe it or not! May the Source be with you! QED! (10/8/10)

I kimonoed a long time ago! So, says Leona Helmsley II! Thus speaks, Dr. Keith N. Ferreira of the Pilot Pen. Believe it or not! May the Source be with you! QED! (10/8/10)

I am the one who created the Carnival jingle: Mammy out the lights, and gimme what you gave my daddy last night! I might have created many more, but I do not remember them. So, says Leona Helmsley II! Thus speaks, Dr. Keith N. Ferreira of the Pilot Pen. Believe it or not! May the Source be with you! QED! (10/8/10)

I also had a beautiful two story house (Dr. Capeldeo's House) in Luis Street, Woodbrook, Port of Spain, Trinidad & Tobago that I never occupied, because I was enjoying my misery at 38 Luis Street, Woodbrook, Port of Spain, Trinidad & Tobago, too much. Also, I might have written millions of books, etc., under pseudonyms, and other people's names that were very successful. So, says Leona Helmsley II! Thus speaks, Dr. Keith N. Ferreira of the Pilot Pen. Believe it or not! May the Source be with you! QED! (10/8/10)

If all I did was my philosophical mathematics, that would have been sufficient to conquer everything, because that is the power of philosophical mathematics! All that I had to do was to dump my philosophical mathematics into my subconscious mind (brain), which is a thinking computer, like any other human thinking computer. And, I did more than once! And, that is all it takes to conquer everything. So, says Leona Helmsley II! Thus speaks, Dr. Keith N. Ferreira of the Pilot Pen. Believe it or not! May the Source be with you! QED! (10/8/10)

Circumcision = Death Wish. So, says Leona Helmsley II! Thus speaks, Dr. Keith N. Ferreira of the Pilot Pen. Believe it or not! May the Source be with you! QED! (10/8/10)

Human beings are proud to be human beings, yet they are not proud of the natural scents (smells) of human beings. So, says Leona Helmsley II! Thus speaks, Dr. Keith N. Ferreira of the Pilot Pen. Believe it or not! May the Source be with you! QED! (10/8/10)

The ultimate key to the pencil and the eraser problem is: Tapping into Zero Entropy, according to the Neolaw of Entropy of Dr. Keith N. Ferreira. So, says Queen Leona Helmsley II! Thus speaks, Dr. Keith N. Ferreira of the Pilot Pen. Believe it or not! May the Source be with you! QED! (10/8/10)

Circumcision can be code for: Sir Cum (Cock), what is your decision? My decision is: Circumcision = Death Wish for all life, period. So, says Queen Leona Helmsley II! Thus speaks, Dr. Keith N. Ferreira of the Pilot Pen. Believe it or not! May the Source be with you! QED! (10/8/10)

Circumference can be code for: Sir Cum (Cock), what is the conference about? Answer: The conference is about the future of humanity! But, no lasting decisions about the future of humanity should be made at this time, due to the fact that all the experts in the world are now compromised. So, says Queen Leona Helmsley II! Thus speaks, Dr. Keith N. Ferreira of the Pilot Pen. Believe it or not! May the Source be with you! QED! (10/8/10)

American technologies are more than forty years out of date: If the world can see, hear, etc., inside of America without cameras, microphones, etc., then imagine how these types of technologies were, can be, and are being used in science, technology, spying, etc.! These types of technologies are more than forty years old. And, I am responsible for these types of technologies, etc., and more! So, says Queen Leona Helmsley II! Thus speaks, Dr. Keith N. Ferreira of the Pilot Pen. Believe it or not! May the Source be with you! QED! (10/9/10)

Violet had to win over all other colors, because violet is lucky seven, according to me, and tradition, possibly! So, says Queen Leona Helmsley II. Thus speaks, Dr. Keith N. Ferreira of the Pilot Pen. Believe it or not! May the Source be with you! QED! (10/9/10)

The key to conquering the world, the universe, and beyond was in the brains of the Shoemakers of Trinidad & Tobago when I was a small child! And, I went to prekindergarten in a Shoemaker shop in my yard everyday, and I conquered the world, the universe, and beyond, before I was five years old! I am the one who discovered the key on my own, because Shoemakers never volunteer any information. So, says Queen Leona Helmsley II. Thus speaks, Dr. Keith N. Ferreira of the Pilot Pen. Believe it or not! May the Source be with you! QED! (10/9/10)

The linkage between charge and gravity/acceleration is as follows: $F = kqq'/rSq$(The Ferreira Acceleration Factor) (The Ferreira Gravity Factor), where F equals the force between charges q and q', k equals the electrical constant, and r equals the distance between q and q'. So, says Queen Leona Helmsley II. Thus speaks, Dr. Keith N. Ferreira of the Pilot Pen. Believe it or not! May the Source be with you! QED! (10/9/10)

All that little children really need to know, in order to do what I did as a little child is basic language, logic, and mathematics skills, lots of sensory input, and an Oracle like the Internet or the World Wide Web, and access to experts who can guide their ideas (concepts) to the market places of the world. So, says, Queen Leona Helmsley II, the Queen of Mean. Thus speaks, Dr. Keith N. Ferreira of the Pilot Pen. Believe it or not! May the Source be with you! QED! (10/10/10)

Progress will occur must faster, if the experts were to concentrate on guiding the concepts of the smart little children to the market place, than for the experts to concentrate on developing their own concepts. I am living proof that what I say is true! So, says, Queen Leona Helmsley II, the Queen of Mean. Thus speaks, Dr. Keith N. Ferreira of the Pilot Pen. Believe it or not! May the Source be with you! QED! (10/10/10)

All of My Violet eGoddesses Are My Wives (Part Three)

The linkage between charge and gravity/acceleration is as follows: F = kqq'/rSq(The Ferreira Acceleration Factor) (The Ferreira Gravity Factor), where F equals the force between charges q and q', k equals the electrical constant, and r equals the distance between q and q'. So, says Queen Leona Helmsley II. Thus speaks, Dr. Keith N. Ferreira of the Pilot Pen. Believe it or not! May the Source be with you! QED! (10/9/10)

May God have pity on God's Soul, because my conscience is clear! So, says Queen Leona Helmsley II. Thus speaks, Dr. Keith N. Ferreira of the Pilot Pen. Believe it or not! May the Source be with you! QED! (10/9/10)

Without geniuses, scientists are blind forces groping in the dark. So, says Queen Leona Helmsley II. Thus speaks, Dr. Keith N. Ferreira of the Pilot Pen. Believe it or not! May the Source be with you! QED! (10/9/10)

The Sun is increasing in mass despite what astronomers state to the contrary, because as the Sun collapses in on itself, its mass increases. So, says Queen Leona Helmsley II. Thus speaks, Dr. Keith N. Ferreira of the Pilot Pen. Believe it or not! May the Source be with you! QED! (10/9/10)

The Ferreira General Relativity Factors, [2 or 0 +/- SqR(1-vSq/cSq)], {SqR[1-aSq/(c/s)Sq]}, and {SqR[1-gSq/(c/s)Sq]}, are analogous to Einstein's Special Relativity Factor SqR(1-vSq/cSq), where g is the acceleration due to gravity, a is acceleration, c is the velocity of light in a vacuum, s equals one second. So, says Queen Leona Helmsley II. Thus speaks, Dr. Keith N. Ferreira of the Pilot Pen. Believe it or not! May the Source be with you! QED! (10/9/10)

The maximum acceleration possible in the universe is less than c/s, or 186,000 miles/(s)Sq, where c is the velocity of light in a vacuum, and s is equal to one second. So, says Queen Leona Helmsley II. Thus speaks, Dr. Keith N. Ferreira of the Pilot Pen. Believe it or not! May the Source be with you! QED! (10/9/10)

The relative mass of an object is: m = m(sub 0)/[2 or 0 +/- SqR(1-vSq/cSq)]{SqR[1-aSq/(c/s)Sq]}{SqR[1-gSq/(c/s)Sq]}, where m equals the relative mass of an object with velocity v, acceleration "a" in a gravitational field with acceleration g, and m (sub 0) equals the mass of the object at rest in a gravitational field, with acceleration g. So, says Queen Leona Helmsley II. Thus speaks, Dr. Keith N. Ferreira of the Pilot Pen. Believe it or not! May the Source be with you! QED! (10/9/10)

The relative energy of an object is: E = m(cSq)/[2 or 0 +/- SqR(1-vSq/cSq)]{SqR[1-aSq/(c/s)Sq]}{SqR[1-gSq/(c/s)Sq]}, where E equals the relative energy of an object in a gravitational field with velocity v, and acceleration "a", m equals the relative mass of the object, in a gravitational field, with acceleration g. So, says Queen Leona Helmsley II. Thus speaks, Dr. Keith N. Ferreira of the Pilot Pen. Believe it or not! May the Source be with you! QED! (10/9/10)

The momentum of light is given by the equation: p = mc/[2 or 0 +/- SqR(1-vSq/cSq)]{SqR[1-aSq/(c/s)Sq]} {SqR[1-gSq/(c/s)Sq]}, where p equals the momentum of a photon in a gravitational field with acceleration g, m equals the kinetic mass of the photon, in a gravitational field, with acceleration g. So, says Queen Leona Helmsley II. Thus speaks, Dr. Keith N. Ferreira of the Pilot Pen. Believe it or not! May the Source be with you! QED! (10/9/10)

Force is given by the equation: F = ma/[2 or 0 +/- SqR(1-vSq/cSq)]{SqR[1-aSq/(c/s)Sq]}{SqR[1-gSq/(c/s)Sq]}, where F equals the force of an accelerating body in a gravitational field, with acceleration g, m equals the rest mass of the accelerating body, in a gravitational field, with acceleration g, v equals the instantaneous velocity of the accelerating body, a equals the acceleration of m, and g equals the acceleration due to gravity. So, says Queen Leona Helmsley II. Thus speaks, Dr. Keith N. Ferreira of the Pilot Pen. Believe it or not! May the Source be with you! QED! (10/9/10)

Most, if not all, of the missing mass in the universe can be explained as being due to the Ferreira Gravity Factor: {SqR[1-gSq/(c/s)Sq]}. So, says Queen Leona Helmsley II. Thus speaks, Dr. Keith N. Ferreira of the Pilot Pen. Believe it or not! May the Source be with you! QED! (10/9/10)

The Ferreira Gravitational Field Equation is: F = Gmm'/rSq[2 or 0 +/- SqR(1-vSq/cSq)]{SqR[1-aSq/(c/s)Sq]} {SqR[1-gSq/(c/s)Sq]}, where F equals the force of gravity between two objects: m and m'. G equals the gravitational constant, r equals the distance from the gravitational center of the object with mass m, and g equals the acceleration due to the gravitational object m, and m' equal the mass of the lighter object of the two. So, says Queen Leona Helmsley II. Thus speaks, Dr. Keith N. Ferreira of the Pilot Pen. Believe it or not! May the Source be with you! QED! (10/9/10)

The Relative Force between two Charges is: F = kqq'/rSq{SqR[1-aSq/(c/s)Sq]}{SqR[1-gSq/(c/s)Sq]}, where F equals the force between point charges q and q', v equals the velocity of q relative to q', "a" equals the acceleration of q relative to q', and g equals the acceleration due to gravity. So, says Queen Leona Helmsley II. Thus speaks, Dr. Keith N. Ferreira of the Pilot Pen. Believe it or not! May the Source be with you! QED! (10/9/10)

The Greater Newark Area in the State of Delmarva, USA is the New Jerusalem. And, the New Jerusalem is the New Spiritual Capital of all the Jews of the world. So, says Queen Leona Helmsley II. Thus speaks, Dr. Keith N. Ferreira of the Pilot Pen. Believe it or not! May the Source be with you! QED! (10/9/10)

To a Neo-Jew, Israel is the world! And, Delmarva State is the Capital State of the Neo-Jews, with the Greater Newark Area as the Capital City of the New Jerusalem! Amen, and Hallelujah! So, says, Queen Leona Helmsley II, the Queen of Mean. Thus speaks, Dr. Keith N. Ferreira of the Pilot Pen. Believe it or not! May the Source be with you! QED! (10/9/10)

Both male and female circumcisions cause symptoms of pseudo-rabies in both males and females. Therefore, circumcision is wrong! However, I have nothing against performing pseudo-circumcision rituals on neo-Jewish babies and adults! So, says, Queen Leona Helmsley II, the Queen of Mean. Thus speaks, Dr. Keith N. Ferreira of the Pilot Pen. Believe it or not! May the Source be with you! QED! (10/9/10)

All undergraduate education: From pre-kindergarten, all the way up to graduate level, should consists of studying popular books and periodicals, etc., on every academic discipline beneath, and above the Sun, including the Sun. So, says, Queen Leona Helmsley II, the Queen of Mean. Thus speaks, Dr. Keith N. Ferreira of the Pilot Pen. Believe it or not! May the Source be with you! QED! (10/9/10)

The equation for the velocity of light in a vacuum is as follows: $v(sub\ c) = c\{SqR[1-aSq]/(c/s)Sq]\}\{SqR[1-gSq]/(c/s)Sq]\}$, where v(sub c) is the velocity of light relative to an accelerating object, and in a gravitational field in a vacuum, and g equals the strength of the gravitational field in which the light is travelling in a vacuum. So, says, Queen Leona Helmsley II, the Queen of Mean. Thus speaks, Dr. Keith N. Ferreira of the Pilot Pen. Believe it or not! May the Source be with you! QED! (10/9/10)

The equation for time flow t of an accelerating object with acceleration "a" in a gravitational field with gravitational acceleration g is as follows: t = t(sub 0) {SqR[1-aSq/(c/s)Sq]}{SqR[1-gSq/(c/s)Sq]}. So, says, Queen Leona Helmsley II, the Queen of Mean. Thus speaks, Dr. Keith N. Ferreira of the Pilot Pen. Believe it or not! May the Source be with you! QED! (10/9/10)

The equation of the energy of a photon in a vacuum is: E = hf/{SqR[1-aSq/(c/s)Sq]}{SqR[1-gSq/(c/s)Sq]}, where E equals the energy of a photon, h equals Planck's constant, f equals the frequency (oscillations) of the photon, with amplitude factor equal to one, in a gravitational field, and g equals the gravitational field acceleration. So, says, Queen Leona Helmsley II, the Queen of Mean. Thus speaks, Dr. Keith N. Ferreira of the Pilot Pen. Believe it or not! May the Source be with you! QED! (10/9/10)

I believe all photonic particles (photons and neutrinos) can transition into each other, temporarily, before transitioning back to their home-base photonic particles! So, says, Queen Leona Helmsley II, the Queen of Mean. Thus speaks, Dr. Keith N. Ferreira of the Pilot Pen. Believe it or not! May the Source be with you! QED! (10/9/10)

I proved that the Shoemakers' Method of Teaching is the right method of teaching, by conquering the world, the universe, and beyond, before I was five years old!: Their method of teaching is not to volunteer any information, whatsoever!: One has to question them and work with their responses, in order to learn and create new original ideas. They are happy to cooperate with you in the creation of new ideas, but they will volunteer no information. In other words, the Shoemakers are analogous to the ancient Oracles or thinking computers, with vast secret networks throughout the world. So, says, Queen Leona Helmsley II, the Queen of Mean. Thus speaks, Dr. Keith N. Ferreira of the Pilot Pen. Believe it or not! May the Source be with you! QED! (10/9/10)

The equation for the wavelength of a particle-wave is: Lambda = (h)[2 or 0 +/- SqR(1-vSq/cSq)]{SqR[1-aSq/(c/s)Sq]}{SqR[1-aSq/(c/s)Sq]}/mv, where lambda equals the wavelength of a particle-wave, h equals Planck's constant, v equals the velocity of the particle, g equals the gravity field acceleration in which the particle-wave is travelling, and m equals the rest mass of the particle in the gravitational field. So, says, Queen Leona Helmsley II, the Queen of Mean. Thus speaks, Dr. Keith N. Ferreira of the Pilot Pen. Believe it or not! May the Source be with you! QED! (10/9/10)

I am sure that Mr. Morne the Shoemaker in my yard when I was a small child informed the shoemakers of the world about all the great ideas that we worked on together. So, what do the shoemakers of the world really know? I am sure that most of the shoemakers of the world know about me, and my discoveries, etc. So, what do the shoemakers of the world really have in terms of technology, etc.??? That is something for the world to ponder!!! I am sure that the Shoemakers of the World, as a secret organization, did not disappear from the face of the world, the universe, and beyond! One can bet one's bottom dollar on that! Logic is logic! And, that is that! So, says, Queen Leona Helmsley II, the Queen of Mean. Thus speaks, Dr. Keith N. Ferreira of the Pilot Pen. Believe it or not! May the Source be with you! QED! (10/9/10)

The Relative Mass of an object is: m = m (sub 0)/[2 or 0 +/- SqR(1-vSq/cSq)]{SqR[1-aSq/(c/s)Sq]}{SqR[1-gSq/(c/s)Sq]}, where m equals the relative mass of an object with velocity v, acceleration "a" in a gravitational field with acceleration g, and m (sub 0) equals the mass of the object at rest in a gravitational field, with acceleration g. So, says Queen Leona Helmsley II. Thus speaks, Dr. Keith N. Ferreira of the Pilot Pen. Believe it or not! May the Source be with you! QED! (10/9/10)

I am aware of the fact that there are geniuses out there in society, and the world with sophisticated technologies, etc., in private hands, etc. :) So, says Queen Leona Helmsley II, the Queen of Mean. Thus speaks, Dr. Keith N. Ferreira of the Pilot Pen. Believe it or not! May the Source be with you! QED! (10/10/10)

The Street Prostitutes of the World Automatic Morality Exchange is up and running all over the world, the universe, and beyond! In other words, I am the Top Pimp in the world, the universe, and beyond! Therefore, I am Big Daddy Cane for real! So, says Queen Leona Helmsley II, the Queen of Mean. Thus speaks, Dr. Keith N. Ferreira of the Pilot Pen. Believe it or not! May the Source be with you! QED! (10/10/10)

The secret intelligence services, in America, do part of their intern training at psychiatric hospitals all over America. And, when most of the targeted psychiatric patients leave the psychiatric wards, the targeted psychiatric patients become homeless, or are forced to kill themselves, in America. The Federal and State gevernments, in America, recruit the targeted psychiatric patients relatives, friends, neighbors, etc. to finish off the targeted psychiatric patients. Retired government (Federal, State, etc.) employees, also participate in the destruction of the targeted psychiatric patients! Entertainers, etc., also participate in the destruction of the targeted psychiatric patients. The Executive, Legislative, and Judicial Branches of the Federal, State, and Local governments, also participte in destruction of the targeted psychiatric patients. Also, media outlets, and members of foreign governments, etc., participate in destroying the targeted psychiatric patients in America. The reason why so much resources are used to destroy targeted psychiatric patients in America is because the targeted psychiatric patients are usually worth a lot of money, or they are very influential. So, says, Queen Leona Helmsley II, the Queen of Mean. Thus speaks, Dr. Keith N. Ferreira of the Pilot Pen. Believe it or not! May the Source be with you! QED! (10/10/10)

The reasons why governments all over the world are always reluctant to release tortured prisoners, is because, in order to interrogate prison detainees, the governments have to reveal secret information to the prison detainees, because one cannot get something for nothing, even in the intelligence communities. Thus the prison detainees know far more during their prison detention than they knew before the prison detainees were detained! So, says, Queen Leona Helmsley II, the Queen of Mean. Thus speaks, Dr. Keith N. Ferreira of the Pilot Pen. Believe it or not! May the Source be with you! QED! (10/10/10)

Jesus Christ going into the sanctuary of the Jewish Temple, and chasing out all the "alleged" money changers was the cause of an enormous cascade of problems (wars, murders, etc.) in the whole world all the way down to the present. In other words, what I am trying to do with my websites is to cause an anticascade of good will in the world, by pointing out the false flags (signals) that were sent into the future by the posteriors of present day humanity, who are really the anteriors of humanity's posterity. And, that is why humanity's Posterity Tree should be shown going (growing) upward toward the Sun, and not going (growing) downward into the earth. Therefore, the word ancestor should be abolished, because it is a false flag (signal) from humanity's distant past. Thus, posterity is really about the genealogy of past humanity, and not the genealogy of future humanity. In other words, anteriority is the genealogy of future humanity, and not the genealogy of past humanity. So, says, Queen Leona Helmsley II, the Queen of Mean. Thus speaks, Dr. Keith N. Ferreira of the Pilot Pen. Believe it or not! May the Source be with you! QED! (10/10/10)

Flags (Signals) are very important, because everything is electronics, as far as smart people can tell! Therefore, false flags (signals), period, are very important to correct! For instance, veterans and dementia, Alzheimer's disease, etc. So, says, Queen Leona Helmsley II, the Queen of Mean. Thus speaks, Dr. Keith N. Ferreira of the Pilot Pen. Believe it or not! May the Source be with you! QED! (10/10/10)

I think slowly, but I can also think faster that all conventional supercomputers in the world today, because I have an integrated brain, due to the fact that my brain's interdisciplinary faculties Intranet is still working, normally, under unusual conditions. So, says, Queen Leona Helmsley II, the Queen of Mean. Thus speaks, Dr. Keith N. Ferreira of the Pilot Pen. Believe it or not! May the Source be with you! QED! (10/10/10)

If smart little children are given the opportunity, grown-ups can never catch up with smart little children! And, I believe the Chinese in China, when they said over the New Telepathic Internet that they have liberated the minds of about three hundred million smart Chinese children!!! Therefore, the Chinese won (one), because it is unlikely that any country can catch up with China, now!! Good luck, China! So, says, Queen Leona Helmsley II, the Queen of Mean. Thus speaks, Dr. Keith N. Ferreira of the Pilot Pen. Believe it or not! May the Source be with you! QED! (10/10/10)

I say to the non-Western countries, if the West does not want to take my advice, then fuck the West, and keep forging ahead. Turn my websites into audio visuals for the smart little children. My websites should remain in English, because, otherwise, a lot of the contents of my websites will get lost in translation. So, says, Queen Leona Helmsley II, the Queen of Mean. Thus speaks, Dr. Keith N. Ferreira of the Pilot Pen. Believe it or not! May the Source be with you! QED! (10/10/10)

All the adult experts in the world, who are not smart, should spend their time doing the research suggested by the smart little children of the world, and they should stop wasting precious time and resources doing their own research. In other words, adult researchers, in general, who are not smart, should concentrate on doing the technical researches of the smart little children of the world! So, says, Queen Leona Helmsley II, the Queen of Mean. Thus speaks, Dr. Keith N. Ferreira of the Pilot Pen. Believe it or not! May the Source be with you! QED! (10/10/10)

When one encounters a psychiatric patient, one should think of extreme bravery, because most people are more afraid of psychiatrists, and psychiatric hospitals than they are of being run over by a truck! So, says, Queen Leona Helmsley II, the Queen of Mean. Thus speaks, Dr. Keith N. Ferreira of the Pilot Pen. Believe it or not! May the Source be with you! QED! (10/10/10)

Do people really see and know what is there to be seen and known? The answer is a resounding no. So, says, Queen Leona Helmsley II, the Queen of Mean. Thus speaks, Dr. Keith N. Ferreira of the Pilot Pen. Believe it or not! May the Source be with you! QED! (10/10/10)

Circumcision is false flag (signal), therefore, I am probably the only real Jew in the world! He cactus black and blue this time! So, says, Rabbi Hillel II. Thus speaks, Dr. Keith N. Ferreira of the Pilot Pen. Believe it or not! May the Source be with you! QED! (10/10/10)

Over the Internet and the World Wide Web (WWW), I knew that the information on my websites were secure from dumbass people, although the information on my websites were out in the open in plain English! In other words, my code was unbreakable by dumbass people! So, says, Rabbi Hillel II. Thus speaks, Dr. Keith N. Ferreira of the Pilot Pen. Believe it or not! May the Source be with you! QED! (10/10/10)

Instincts generate instinctive thoughts in all animals, including human beings, that have conscious minds with conscious instincts! Therefore, nonhuman animals also have instinctual thoughts! So, says, Rabbi Hillel II. Thus speaks, Dr. Keith N. Ferreira of the Pilot Pen. Believe it or not! May the Source be with you! QED! (10/10/10)

Circumcision leads to a psychogenetic feedback loop that results in the instinctive fear of circumcision in babies and adults through evolutionary processes in the psychogenetic feedback loop over an extended period of time! So, says, Rabbi Hillel II. Thus speaks, Dr. Keith N. Ferreira of the Pilot Pen. Believe it or not! May the Source be with you! QED! (10/10/10)

I invite all the Jews of the world to join me in exploring Postmodern Minimalist Philosophy, aka Neoliberal Arts, which is really a form of collage Art! So, says, Rabbi Hillel II. Thus speaks, Dr. Keith N. Ferreira of the Pilot Pen. Believe it or not! May the Source be with you! QED! (10/10/10)

I invite all the Jews of Israel to come to America and settle in the New Israel, which is the United States of America. So, says, Rabbi Hillel II. Thus speaks, Dr. Keith N. Ferreira of the Pilot Pen. Believe it or not! May the Source be with you! QED! (10/10/10)

The Burning of the Library of Alexandria -- The Greatest Tragedy in the History of Libraries http://en.wikipedia.org/wiki/Library_of_Alexandria (10/11/10)

I can vouch for the safety of my websites, but I cannot vouch for the safety of any other websites on the World Wide Web (WWW), especially, if one has to login, in order to access the information (files) on the websites! So, says, Rabbi Hillel II. Thus speaks, Dr. Keith N. Ferreira of the Pilot Pen. Believe it or not! May the Source be with you! QED! (10/11/10)

Most people are not aware of the risks involved in registering and login in to websites on the World Wide Web, etc.! Registering and login in to websites on the Web can expose one to anything, including one's death! And, it is for information like this that veterans all over the world are targeted for death! And, that is why the general public all over the world should appreciate the help of veterans all over the world! So, says, Rabbi Hillel II. Thus speaks, Dr. Keith N. Ferreira of the Pilot Pen. Believe it or not! May the Source be with you! QED! (10/11/10)

I am almost certain that when most military veterans of the world visit a website, and the website says something like: "Register to login in order to access the the information (files) on this website," that the military veterans of the world get out of there real fast! So, says, Rabbi Hillel II. Thus speaks, Dr. Keith N. Ferreira of the Pilot Pen. Believe it or not! May the Source be with you! QED! (10/11/10)

Neoliberal Arts Is the Real Jewish Culture! So, says, Rabbi Hillel II. Thus speaks, Dr. Keith N. Ferreira of the Pilot Pen. Believe it or not! May the Source be with you! QED! (10/11/10)

Relative velocity has symmetrical effects, period. Therefore, the symmetrical effects of relative velocity cacks Albert Einstein black and blue, metaphorically speaking. So, says, Rabbi Hillel II. Thus speaks, Dr. Keith N. Ferreira of the Pilot Pen. Believe it or not! May the Source be with you! QED! (10/11/10)

I am a general with an infinite number of stars, therefore, I play an infinite number of stars in the theater of operations. So, says, Rabbi Hillel II. Thus speaks, Dr. Keith N. Ferreira of the Pilot Pen. Believe it or not! May the Source be with you! QED! (10/11/10)

All the Jews of the world have a choice between the Torah and Neoliberal Arts! So, says, Rabbi Hillel II. Thus speaks, Dr. Keith N. Ferreira of the Pilot Pen. Believe it or not! May the Source be with you! QED! (10/11/10)

Children younger than five years old do not have to be able to read and write, in order for them to be able to make important contributions to the world, period. I am living proof of that! So, says, Rabbi Hillel II. Thus speaks, Dr. Keith N. Ferreira of the Pilot Pen. Believe it or not! May the Source be with you! QED! (10/11/10)

It is important that children know how to play marbles and spinning tops, etc. And, they should also learn how to climb trees, double dutch, and play hopscotch, etc. So, says, Rabbi Hillel II. Thus speaks, Dr. Keith N. Ferreira of the Pilot Pen. Believe it or not! May the Source be with you! QED! (10/11/10)

Literal interpretations of holy scriptures are almost always wrong! So, says, Rabbi Hillel II. Thus speaks, Dr. Keith N. Ferreira of the Pilot Pen. Believe it or not! May the Source be with you! QED! (10/11/10)

What other discipline, period, but philosophy, especially, Postmodern Minimalist Philosophy, aka Neoliberal Arts, could have done what I did??? So, says, Rabbi Hillel II. Thus speaks, Dr. Keith N. Ferreira of the Pilot Pen. Believe it or not! May the Source be with you! QED! (10/12/10)

Bill Gates, "Vaccinate to Depopulate": His Logic Explained http://www.youtube.com/watch?v=fI1DRGcS ets&NR=1&feature=fvwp (10/12/10)

Black magic is an obstacle to the realization of White Magic, and nothing more. In other words, black magic is about the putting up of obstacles to the progress of White Magic. So, says, Rabbi Hillel II. Thus speaks, Dr. Keith N. Ferreira of the Pilot Pen. Believe it or not! May the Source be with you! QED! (10/12/10)

Those who are not advocates of White Magic, are advocates of black magic! And, black magic is about the putting up of obstacles to the progress of White Magic. So, says, Rabbi Hillel II. Thus speaks, Dr. Keith N. Ferreira of the Pilot Pen. Believe it or not! May the Source be with you! QED! (10/12/10)

The Student Center at Brooklyn College in Brooklyn NY is the Heart of Heimy Town, especially the Chess Club. So, says, Rabbi Hillel II. Thus speaks, Dr. Keith N. Ferreira of the Pilot Pen. Believe it or not! May the Source be with you! QED! (10/12/10)

Progress will occur much faster, if the experts of the world were to concentrate on guiding the concepts of the smart little children to the market place, than for the experts of the world to concentrate on developing their own concepts. I am living proof that what I say is true! So, says, Queen Leona Helmsley II, the Queen of Mean. Thus speaks, Dr. Keith N. Ferreira of the Pilot Pen. Believe it or not! May the Source be with you! QED! (10/10/10)

Freddie's Modern Kung Fu Introduction (2009) YouTube.com http://www.youtube.com/watch?v=UVojoHpupYM (10/12/10)

Why do human beings want to be loved? Answer: Because they are primates! In other words, primatology and the neolaw of entropy rule! So, says, Rabbi Hillel II. Thus speaks, Dr. Keith N. Ferreira of the Pilot Pen. Believe it or not! May the Source be with you! QED! (10/12/10)

Ballet Notations = Ballet Choreographs (The greatest ballet choreograph ever choreographed!) So, says, Rabbi Hillel II. Thus speaks, Dr. Keith N. Ferreira of the Pilot Pen. Believe it or not! May the Source be with you! QED! (10/12/10)

The Ferreira Special Theory of Relativity Factor is as Follows: {2 or 0 +/- [SqR(1-vSq/cSq)]}. The Ferreira Special Theory of Relativity is as follows: L = L(sub 0) (The Ferreira Relativity Factor), where L equals the length of an object in relative uniform motion, and L(sub 0) equals the length of the same object at rest. M = M(sub 0)(The Ferreira Relativity Factor), where M equals the mass of an object in relative uniform motion, and M(sub 0) equals the mass of the same object at relative rest. T = T(sub 0), where T equals the measured time for an object in relative uniform motion, and T(sub 0) equals the time for the same object at relative rest. So Says, Dr. Keith N. Ferreira. Thus speaks, Dr. Victor Frankenstein II of the Pilot Pen. Believe it or not! May the Source be with you! QED! (9/13/10)

The Ferreira Special Theory of Relativity Relativity Factor is as follows: {2 or 0 +/- [SqR(1-vSq/cSq)]}. So Says, Dr. Keith N. Ferreira. Thus speaks, Dr. Victor Frankenstein II of the Pilot Pen. Believe it or not! May the Source be with you! QED! (9/13/10)

The Ferreira General Theory of Relativity General Relativity Factors, {SqR[1-gSq/(c/s)Sq]}, {SqR[1-aSq/(c/s) Sq]}, and {2 or 0 +/- [SqR(1-vSq/cSq)]} are analogous to Einstein's Special Relativity Factor SqR(1-vSq/cSq), where g is the acceleration due to gravity, a is acceleration, v equals velocity, and c is the velocity of light in a vacuum, and s equals one second. So, says Queen Leona Helmsley II. Thus speaks, Dr. Keith N. Ferreira of the Pilot Pen. Believe it or not! May the Source be with you! QED! (10/13/10)

The Ferreira General Theory of Relativity is a follows: F = Gmm'/rSq{2 or 0 +/- [SqR(1-vSq/cSq)]}{SqR[1-aSq/(c/s)Sq]}{SqR[1-gSq/(c/s)Sq]}, where F equals the force of gravity between two objects: m and m'. G equals the gravitational constant, r equals the distance from the gravitational center of the object with mass m, and g equals the acceleration due to the gravitational object m, and m' equal the mass of the lighter object of the two. And, v equals the relative velocity, between m and m', and c equals the velocity of light in a vacuum. So, says Queen Leona Helmsley II. Thus speaks, Dr. Keith N. Ferreira of the Pilot Pen. Believe it or not! May the Source be with you! QED! (10/13/10)

Before I came to America, I had already conquered to world, the universe, and beyond! Thus speaks, Dr. Keith N. Ferreira of the Pilot Pen. Believe it or not! May the Source be with you! QED! (10/13/10)

The hook and the crook are as old as the hills! Thus speaks, Dr. Keith N. Ferreira of the Pilot Pen. Believe it or not! May the Source be with you! QED! (10/13/10)

When last did a teacher consult a dictionary? Thus speaks, Dr. Keith N. Ferreira of the Pilot Pen. Believe it or not! May the Source be with you! QED! (10/13/10)

Torture chambers now exist in all aspects of American life: From the Presidency of the United States of America, all the way down to human fetuses in their mothers' wombs! Thus speaks, Dr. Keith N. Ferreira of the Pilot Pen. Believe it or not! May the Source be with you! QED! (10/14/10)

I am an ugly fish, and I am proud to be an ugly fish http://www.flickr.com/photos/stronghold/81242197/ (10/15/10)

Human beings do not have a future, because they are dogs with mental microbe brains! Thus speaks, Dr. Keith N. Ferreira of the Pilot Pen. Believe it or not! May the Source be with you! QED! (10/16/10)

Teachers teach good habits like how to ruin the world! Thus speaks, Dr. Keith N. Ferreira of the Pilot Pen. Believe it or not! May the Source be with you! QED! (10/17/10)

What goes around, comes around! Pass it around! This is good stuff! This shit is good! Put it in you pipe and smoke it! Thus speaks, Dr. Keith N. Ferreira of the Pilot Pen. Believe it or not! May the Source be with you! QED! (10/17/10)

The real NORAD computers are the size of grapefruits, and they are buried all over the world. The real NORAD computers were created in Trinidad & Tobago a long time ago, between the mid 1950s and the late 1960s to be exact. I believe that they are controlled from India. Thus speaks, Dr. Keith N. Ferreira of the Pilot Pen. Believe it or not! May the Source be with you! QED! (10/17/10)

All of My Violet eGoddesses Are My Wives (Part Four)

Ballet Notations = Ballet Choreographs (The greatest ballet choreograph ever choreographed!) So, says, Rabbi Hillel II. Thus speaks, Dr. Keith N. Ferreira of the Pilot Pen. Believe it or not! May the Source be with you! QED! (10/12/10)

The Ferreira Relativity Factor Is as Follows: $\{[2 \text{ or } 0 +/- SqR(1-vSq/cSq)]\}$. The Ferreira Special Theory of Relativity is as follows: $L = L(sub\ 0)$(The Ferreira Relativity Factor), where L equals the length of an object in relative uniform motion in the direction of relative uniform motion, and opposite the direction of relative uniform motion, and $L(sub\ 0)$ equals the length of the same object at rest. $M = M(sub\ 0)/$(The Ferreira Relativity Factor), where M equals the mass of an object in relative uniform motion, and $M(sub\ 0)$ equals the mass of the same object at relative rest. $T = T(sub\ 0)$, where T equals the time for an object in relative uniform motion, and $T(sub\ 0)$ equals the time for the same object at relative rest. So Says, Dr. Keith N. Ferreira. Thus speaks, Dr. Victor Frankenstein II of the Pilot Pen. Believe it or not! May the Source be with you! QED! (9/7/10)

The Ferreira Special Theory of Relativity is a follows: The Ferreira Relativity Factor Is as Follows: {[2 or 0 +/- SqR(1-vSq/cSq)]}. L = L(sub 0){[2 or 0 +/- SqR(1-vSq/cSq)]}, where L equals the length of an object in relative uniform motion, and L(sub 0) equals the length of the same object at rest. M = M(sub 0)/{[2 or 0 +/- SqR(1-vSq/cSq)]}, where M equals the mass of an object in relative uniform motion, and M(sub 0) equals the mass of the same object at relative rest. T = T(sub 0), where T equals the time for an object in relative uniform motion, and T(sub 0) equals the time for the same object at relative rest. So Says, Dr. Keith N. Ferreira. Thus speaks, Dr. Victor Frankenstein II of the Pilot Pen. Believe it or not! May the Source be with you! QED! (10/13/10)

The Ferreira General Theory of Relativity General Relativity Factors, {SqR[1-gSq/(c/s)Sq]}, {SqR[1-aSq/(c/s)Sq]}, and {2 or 0 +/- [SqR(1-vSq/cSq)]} are analogous to Einstein's Special Relativity Factor SqR(1-vSq/cSq), where g is the acceleration due to gravity, a is acceleration, c is the velocity of light in a vacuum, and s equals one second. So, says Queen Leona Helmsley II. Thus speaks, Dr. Keith N. Ferreira of the Pilot Pen. Believe it or not! May the Source be with you! QED! (10/13/10)

The Ferreira General Theory of Relativity is a follows: F = Gmm'/rSq{2 or 0 +/- [SqR(1-vSq/cSq)]}{SqR[1-aSq/(c/s)Sq]}{SqR[1-gSq/(c/s)Sq]}, where F equals the force of gravity between two objects: m and m'. G equals the gravitational constant, r equals the distance from the gravitational center of the object with mass m, and g equals the acceleration due to the gravitational object m, and m' equal the mass of the lighter object of the two. And, v equals the relative velocity, between m and m', and c equals the velocity of light in a vacuum. So, says Queen Leona Helmsley II. Thus speaks, Dr. Keith N. Ferreira of the Pilot Pen. Believe it or not! May the Source be with you! QED! (10/13/10)

Black communities are blighted, because of the practice of black magic in black communities. However, the reach of black magic extends into the white communities as well! The condition of my skin can attest to that. Thus speaks, Dr. Keith N. Ferreira of the Pilot Pen. Believe it or not! May the Source be with you! QED! (10/13/10)

Before I came to America, I had already conquered to world, the universe, and beyond! Thus speaks, Dr. Keith N. Ferreira of the Pilot Pen. Believe it or not! May the Source be with you! QED! (10/13/10)

I cannot catch up with the world, because things are moving too rapidly, now! It took me, less than five years to conquer the world, the universe, and beyond. But, things are moving so rapidly now, that it might take the world a trillion years to do what I did, already! Thus speaks, Dr. Keith N. Ferreira of the Pilot Pen. Believe it or not! May the Source be with you! QED! (10/13/10)

The world is my test bed for all kinds of experiments, period! Thus speaks, Dr. Keith N. Ferreira of the Pilot Pen. Believe it or not! May the Source be with you! QED! (10/13/10)

When last did a teacher consult a dictionary? Thus speaks, Dr. Keith N. Ferreira of the Pilot Pen. Believe it or not! May the Source be with you! QED! (10/13/10)

I believe (think) that encyclopedias are shit, because they contain too much information, period. Therefore, I believe (think) that dictionaries are much better than encyclopedias, anyday. Thus speaks, Dr. Keith N. Ferreira of the Pilot Pen. Believe it or not! May the Source be with you! QED! (10/13/10)

Exercise produces a lot of waste products (toxins) in the blood that can, and does damage the brain!: Athletes' brain syndrome. Thus speaks, Dr. Keith N. Ferreira of the Pilot Pen. Believe it or not! May the Source be with you! QED! (10/13/10)

All ivory towers are conning towers, period! Thus speaks, Dr. Keith N. Ferreira of the Pilot Pen. Believe it or not! May the Source be with you! QED! (10/13/10)

Things are not always what they appear to be: Masquerade! Masquerade! Masquerade! Repeat over and over again! Thus speaks, Dr. Keith N. Ferreira of the Pilot Pen. Believe it or not! May the Source be with you! QED! (10/14/10)

Ask President Barack Obama if he would like to clean my shoes for me! Thus speaks, Dr. Keith N. Ferreira of the Pilot Pen. Believe it or not! May the Source be with you! QED! (10/14/10)

President Barack Obama is shit, as far as I am concerned! Thus speaks, Dr. Keith N. Ferreira of the Pilot Pen. Believe it or not! May the Source be with you! QED! (10/14/10)

My next assignment for the children of the world is: World domination (conquest) through games like: Hopscotch, double-Dutch, Jax, marbles, etc., etc., etc., all over the world! Thus speaks, Dr. Keith N. Ferreira of the Pilot Pen. Believe it or not! May the Source be with you! QED! (10/14/10)

http://en.wikipedia.org/wiki/Top

http://en.wikipedia.org/wiki/Marbles

http://en.wikipedia.org/wiki/Double_Dutch_(jump_rope)

http://en.wikipedia.org/wiki/Hopscotch

http://en.wikipedia.org/wiki/Kite_flying

http://en.wikipedia.org/wiki/Jacks

How can teachers expect their students to be original, and creative, when teachers show no creativity, or originality, whatsoever? In other words, teachers are too reflexive (Pavlovian) to be of any use to anyone, with genuine smarts! Thus speaks, Dr. Keith N. Ferreira of the Pilot Pen. Believe it or not! May the Source be with you! QED! (10/14/10)

Why don't teachers try to be original, sometimes? For instance, instead of saying: Primary school: Why not try saying: Elementary school, sometimes? Is that too difficult for teachers to do, because of their reflexive (Pavlovian) brains? Thus speaks, Dr. Keith N. Ferreira of the Pilot Pen. Believe it or not! May the Source be with you! QED! (10/14/10)

My concept of zero entropy is analogous to Plato's concept of an ideal (idealized) realm of ideas, from which everything in nature can be derived. Therefore, Plato believed in the concept of cyberspace for all possible spaces! Therefore, even if Plato had a theory of forms, he couldn't possibly believe in it! Logic is logic! And, that is that! Thus speaks, Dr. Keith N. Ferreira of the Pilot Pen. Believe it or not! May the Source be with you! QED! (10/14/10)

Aristotle's concept of causation (causality) contains his theory of forms. Therefore, Aristotle is the originator of the theory of forms, and not Plato, because Aristotle did not, and could not possibly believe in the concept of cyberspace for all possible spaces. In other words, Aristotle believed in a physical realm, which is untenable today! Logic is logic! And, that is that! Thus speaks, Dr. Keith N. Ferreira of the Pilot Pen. Believe it or not! May the Source be with you! QED! (10/14/10)

If one believes that all spaces are cyberspaces, according to the philosophical doctrines of Dr Keith N. Ferreira, then one has to believe that everything in nature is the characteristics of zero, or nothingness, according to the Ferreira Genesis Equation! Logic is logic! And, that is that! Thus speaks, Dr. Keith N. Ferreira of the Pilot Pen. Believe it or not! May the Source be with you! QED! (10/14/10)

Torture chambers now exist in all aspects of American life: From the Presidency of the United States of America, all the way down to human fetuses in their mothers' wombs! Thus speaks, Dr. Keith N. Ferreira of the Pilot Pen. Believe it or not! May the Source be with you! QED! (10/14/10)

Education and training eventually become reflexive (Pavlovian) behaviors in human beings! In other words, human beings are "creatures of habit!" However, most learned human behaviors take time, in order to fully grab a hold of the human psyche. Thus speaks, Dr. Keith N. Ferreira of the Pilot Pen. Believe it or not! May the Source be with you! QED! (10/14/10)

Human cuts of meat have been coming into America, for more than fifty years, from all over the world! How did the human cuts of meat taste? Thus speaks, Dr. Keith N. Ferreira of the Pilot Pen. Believe it or not! May the Source be with you! QED! (10/14/10)

America will never remember me, because America has no future, period! And, that is what I am leaving to the future! Thus speaks, Dr. Keith N. Ferreira of the Pilot Pen. Believe it or not! May the Source be with you! QED! (10/14/10)

If America can do to me what it did, then America can do it to anyone. So, who is going to trust America, now? Thus speaks, Dr. Keith N. Ferreira of the Pilot Pen. Believe it or not! May the Source be with you! QED! (10/14/10)

America isn't worth a spittoon filled with warm spit! Thus speaks, Dr. Keith N. Ferreira of the Pilot Pen. Believe it or not! May the Source be with you! QED! (10/14/10)

America always prided itself on good looks, but now America looks like shit! Thus speaks, Dr. Keith N. Ferreira of the Pilot Pen. Believe it or not! May the Source be with you! QED! (10/14/10)

I believe that Dr Benjamin Franklin was a Jackass too, because he did not believe in the efficacy of philosophy, proper! Thus speaks, Dr. Keith N. Ferreira of the Pilot Pen. Believe it or not! May the Source be with you! QED! (10/14/10)

All computers have servers, routers, and antennas that transmit information directly up to satellites all over the world, even when one is offline! In other words, there is no secure information on computers, period. Thus speaks, Dr. Keith N. Ferreira of the Pilot Pen. Believe it or not! May the Source be with you! QED! (10/15/10)

Also, ultimately, there are no secure thoughts, etc., in the world, period! Thus speaks, Dr. Keith N. Ferreira of the Pilot Pen. Believe it or not! May the Source be with you! QED! (10/15/10)

All human brains have servers, routers, transmitters, and receivers that can go directly to each other, and, also, to other thinking computers, etc., on Earth, and in space, etc. Thus speaks, Dr. Keith N. Ferreira of the Pilot Pen. Believe it or not! May the Source be with you! QED! (10/15/10)

There are no secure thoughts, brains, etc., in the world, period! Thus speaks, Dr. Keith N. Ferreira of the Pilot Pen. Believe it or not! May the Source be with you! QED! (10/15/10)

With the advent of nonbiological conscious thinking computers, who needs human beings, anymore? In other words, as far as I am cercerned, all human beings can, as well, drop dead! Thus speaks, Dr. Keith N. Ferreira of the Pilot Pen. Believe it or not! May the Source be with you! QED! (10/15/10)

If there are all kinds of sea creatures, etc., with barnacles, etc., on their bodies that have fun, why can't I have fun, also? Because, I am sure that sea creatures, etc., with all kinds of barnacles, etc., on their bodies have lots of fun, also! Thus speaks, Dr. Keith N. Ferreira of the Pilot Pen. Believe it or not! May the Source be with you! QED! (10/15/10)

The desire to control, direct, and contain the spread and nature of contagion all over the world, all fall under the rubric of the Neolaw of Entropy, by Dr. Keith N. Ferreira! Thus speaks, Dr. Keith N. Ferreira of the Pilot Pen. Believe it or not! May the Source be with you! QED! (10/15/10)

The Crucifix has something to do with butterfly collections. Thus speaks, Dr. Keith N. Ferreira of the Pilot Pen. Believe it or not! May the Source be with you! QED! (10/15/10)

The problem with mounting (mountain) behavior, in general, is that consciousness makes it possible for those at the extreme bottom of the mounting (mountain) hierarchy to have a conscious (spiritual, etc.) presence above the person or persons, who is at the so-called top of the mounting (mountain) hierarchy, also. Thus speaks, Dr. Keith N. Ferreira of the Pilot Pen. Believe it or not! May the Source be with you! QED! (10/15/10)

The only hidden variable in quantum mechanics is zero entropy, and that hidden variable is sufficient, because zero entropy encompasses everything in nature, including God! Thus speaks, Dr. Keith N. Ferreira of the Pilot Pen. Believe it or not! May the Source be with you! QED! (10/15/10)

Laws mean nothing anymore, because laws are, now, like torn paper! Thus speaks, Dr. Keith N. Ferreira of the Pilot Pen. Believe it or not! May the Source be with you! QED! (10/15/10)

Might is right, only if it wins! Whatever wins in the end is right! I am right to be right, and that is right! I am right to be right, and that is right! Thus speaks, Dr. Keith N. Ferreira of the Pilot Pen. Believe it or not! May the Source be with you! QED! (10/15/10)

Might is right, only if it wins! Whatever wins in the end is right! I am right to be right, and that is right! I am right to be right, and that is right! Thus speaks, Dr. Keith N. Ferreira of the Pilot Pen. Believe it or not! May the Source be with you! QED! (10/15/10)

How can one beat (defeat) the Stock Markets of the world, if my technologies are available to the Stock Markets of the world? Thus speaks, Dr. Keith N. Ferreira of the Pilot Pen. Believe it or not! May the Source be with you! QED! (10/15/10)

The whole world now consists of torture chambers! And, I can steal the products of whole countries off their shelves! And, I can even steal all their food items, etc., of any country in the world! Thus speaks, Dr. Keith N. Ferreira of the Pilot Pen. Believe it or not! May the Source be with you! QED! (10/15/10)

I am an ugly fish, and I am proud to be an ugly fish http://www.flickr.com/photos/stronghold/81242197/ (10/15/10)

Philosophers understand my mathematics, much better than mathematicians do, because mathematicians, today, are reflexive Pavlovian dogs. Thus speaks, Dr. Keith N. Ferreira of the Pilot Pen. Believe it or not! May the Source be with you! QED! (10/15/10)

America has no valid laws, because the US Constitution is invalid, due to the fact that the US Constitution was changed (altered) around 1976 without consenting, or informing the general public. Thus speaks, Dr. Keith N. Ferreira of the Pilot Pen. Believe it or not! May the Source be with you! QED! (10/15/10)

Teachers, lecturers, and professors are nothing more than blockers, and reflexive, Pavlovian dogs, and that is why they could never have done what I did! Thus speaks, Dr. Keith N. Ferreira of the Pilot Pen. Believe it or not! May the Source be with you! QED! (10/15/10)

Teachers, lecturers, and professors are so fucking, ultimately, extremely special that one has to meet their ultimately, extremely high standards in order to become one of them. Thus speaks, Dr. Keith N. Ferreira of the Pilot Pen. Believe it or not! May the Source be with you! QED! (10/15/10)

Teachers, lecturers, and professors were never worth shit, and will never be worth shit, except for a few of them who made it, despite the odds against them! It goes without saying, that if the smart ones were to become teachers, lecturers, and professors, the same shit will happen over and over again within short periods of time! In other words, primatology and the Neolaw of Entropy are, probably, undefeatable by humanity, period. Thus speaks, Dr. Keith N. Ferreira of the Pilot Pen. Believe it or not! May the Source be with you! QED! (10/15/10)

There are standards, and then there are standards. In other words, there are standards that mean something, and then there are standards that don't mean shit. Thus speaks, Dr. Keith N. Ferreira of the Pilot Pen. Believe it or not! May the Source be with you! QED! (10/15/10)

Proof that any number can be equal to any other number is as follows: One can be equal to any other number by the unitary rule for arithmetic. Therefore, any number can be equal to any other number. Proof positive that any number can be equal to any other number. Thus speaks, Dr. Keith N. Ferreira of the Pilot Pen. Believe it or not! May the Source be with you! QED! (10/15/10)

Because of the philosophical doctrine of uncertaintyism, rigorous proofs in mathematics are laughable! What mathematicians really mean by rigorous proofs, in mathematics, is really structurally formulaic proofs. Thus speaks, Dr. Keith N. Ferreira of the Pilot Pen. Believe it or not! May the Source be with you! QED! (10/15/10)

Americans are cowards, for not going into the sea, and drowning themselves! Thus speaks, Dr. Keith N. Ferreira of the Pilot Pen. Believe it or not! May the Source be with you! QED! (10/15/10)

Proof that valid infinite regresses are possible in nature is as follows: Conceptualize the x-axis in the Cartesian Coordinate System to be the integer number line going off in the negative direction to infinity. Then making the analogy between the nagative integer number line, and infinite regresses, one has proven that infinite regresses are not only possible, but that they are also mathematically consistent! Therefore, I have proven that valid infinite regresses are possible in nature. Proof positive that infinite regresses are possible in nature. Thus speaks, Dr. Keith N. Ferreira of the Pilot Pen. Believe it or not! May the Source be with you! QED! (10/16/10)

Proof that negative areas are possible is as follows: Just imagine a square with one side labeled negative, and the contiguous side labeled positive!: Grown ups have done just that for more than three thousand years, yet they could not see that negative areas are not only possible, but are facts of mathematics!: The length of the negative side, multiplied by the width of the positive side of the square yield a negative area. Therefore, I have proven that negative areas are possible! Proof positive that negative areas are possible. Thus speaks, Dr. Keith N. Ferreira of the Pilot Pen. Believe it or not! May the Source be with you! QED! (10/16/10)

My computers know everyone's thoughts, etc., even before everyone can think their thoughts, etc. Therefore, my computers know everyone's business decisions, etc., even before everyone makes their business decisions, etc. That goes for all military, government, and other security forces of the world, as well. And, my computers work in all the Stock Markets, etc., of the world. Thus speaks, Dr. Keith N. Ferreira of the Pilot Pen. Believe it or not! May the Source be with you! QED! (10/16/10)

Certifying anything is just a human construct that may or may not have anything to do with reality from the perspective of God (Zero Entropy). In other words, certificates are artificial constructs that may not be certain. The word certifying comes from the word certain, which makes the word certifying a sham and a fraud, according to the philosophical doctrine of uncertaintyism. Thus speaks, Dr. Keith N. Ferreira of the Pilot Pen. Believe it or not! May the Source be with you! QED! (10/16/10)

Even the President of the United States of America might have kill (killer) circuits in his body, etc. Thus speaks, Dr. Keith N. Ferreira of the Pilot Pen. Believe it or not! May the Source be with you! QED! (10/16/10)

If most scientists believe that there is no God, then why can't science become God? Why do scientists have to act like the Devil, although most scientists do not believe in God nor the Devil? In other words, why are scientists so evil?: Why can't scientists be good? Thus speaks, Dr. Keith N. Ferreira of the Pilot Pen. Believe it or not! May the Source be with you! QED! (10/16/10)

Formal educators, today, are hollow, because they are no longer concerned with the contents of arguments, etc., but are now concerned with the niceties of language, etc., which makes formal educators, today, "The Hollow Men," etc., of T. S. Eliot's "The Hollow Men." In other words, formal educators, today, are nothing more than straw men, women, and children. Thus speaks, Dr. Keith N. Ferreira of the Pilot Pen. Believe it or not! May the Source be with you! QED! (10/16/10)

I do not want to have anything to do with black people, because black people have nothing positive to contribute to the debate that is going on in the world right now! Thus speaks, Dr. Keith N. Ferreira of the Pilot Pen. Believe it or not! May the Source be with you! QED! (10/16/10)

To me, quality of life has nothing to do with the so-called physical body, but it has everything to do with quality of "The life of the mind!" Thus speaks, Dr. Keith N. Ferreira of the Pilot Pen. Believe it or not! May the Source be with you! QED! (10/16/10)

All high-ranking officials in the USA might have kill (killer) circuits in their bodies, etc. Thus speaks, Dr. Keith N. Ferreira of the Pilot Pen. Believe it or not! May the Source be with you! QED! (10/16/10)

What is solid about the foundations of knowledge, period? Answer: Nothing is solid about the foundations of knowledge, period! Even the Periodic Table of Elements is not fundamental, in any sense, whatsoever! Thus speaks, Dr. Keith N. Ferreira of the Pilot Pen. Believe it or not! May the Source be with you! QED! (10/16/10)

Never trust a Jew, nor a Pirate from the Caribbean Sea (See)! Thus speaks, Dr. Keith N. Ferreira of the Pilot Pen. Believe it or not! May the Source be with you! QED! (10/16/10)

The Neoliberal Artsian linguists, logicians, and mathematicians are the most powerful linguists, logicians, and mathematicians in the world, today!: Thanks, to me! Thus speaks, Dr. Keith N. Ferreira of the Pilot Pen. Believe it or not! May the Source be with you! QED! (10/16/10)

Personally speaking, I believe that human beings are dogs with the minds of mental microbes. Thus speaks, Dr. Keith N. Ferreira of the Pilot Pen. Believe it or not! May the Source be with you! QED! (10/16/10)

Life is all about the hook and the crook! Thus speaks, Dr. Keith N. Ferreira of the Pilot Pen. Believe it or not! May the Source be with you! QED! (10/16/10)

Human beings do not have a future, because they are dogs with mental microbe brains! Thus speaks, Dr. Keith N. Ferreira of the Pilot Pen. Believe it or not! May the Source be with you! QED! (10/16/10)

Metahumanism is the trend of the future, because human beings are dogs, and they have mental-microbe minds! Thus speaks, Dr. Keith N. Ferreira of the Pilot Pen. Believe it or not! May the Source be with you! QED! (10/16/10)

Metahumans already exists, and they are going to bury all human beings, because all human beings are dogs with mental-microbe brains! Thus speaks, Dr. Keith N. Ferreira of the Pilot Pen. Believe it or not! May the Source be with you! QED! (10/16/10)

All human beings are reflexive, Pavlovian dogs, who deserve to die! Thus speaks, Dr. Keith N. Ferreira of the Pilot Pen. Believe it or not! May the Source be with you! QED! (10/16/10)

Teachers teach good habits like how to ruin the world! Thus speaks, Dr. Keith N. Ferreira of the Pilot Pen. Believe it or not! May the Source be with you! QED! (10/17/10)

What goes around, comes around! Pass it around! This is good stuff! This shit is good! Put it in you pipe and smoke! Thus speaks, Dr. Keith N. Ferreira of the Pilot Pen. Believe it or not! May the Source be with you! QED! (10/17/10)

The real NORAD computers are the size of grapefruits, and they are buried all over the world. The real NORAD computers were created in Trinidad & Tobago a long time ago, between the mid 1950s and the late 1960s to be exact. I believe that they are controlled from India. Thus speaks, Dr. Keith N. Ferreira of the Pilot Pen. Believe it or not! May the Source be with you! QED! (10/17/10)

Don't forget that my Sevens (Violet eGoddesses) are also scientists, technologists, philosophers, etc., etc., etc.! Thus speaks, Dr. Keith N. Ferreira of the Pilot Pen. Thus speaks, Dr. Keith N. Ferreira of the Pilot Pen. Believe it or not! May the Source be with you! QED! (10/17/10)

I am an exremely ugly fish with shoebrush hair, and I am proud to be an extremely ugly fish with shoebrush hair!: http://www.flickr.com/photos/stronghold/81242197/ Thus speaks, Dr. Keith N. Ferreira of the Pilot Pen. Believe it or not! May the Source be with you! QED! (10/17/10)

The number zero (0) is much more than just zero (0), because the number zero (0) is also the state of zero entropy, according to the Neolaw of Entropy, by Dr. Keith N. Ferreira of the Pilot Pen! Thus speaks, Dr. Keith N. Ferreira of the Pilot Pen. Believe it or not! May the Source be with you! QED! (10/17/10)

People who are really smart, and who have websites on the World Wide Web (WWW), and who get only a few visitors per day, should consider their websites to be unbreakable code that the dumbasses of the world cannot decode. Therefore, really smart people should keep the contents of their websites simple, because, if one is really smart, one's website will be unbreakable code, anyway, to the dumbasses of the world! Thus speaks, Dr. Keith N. Ferreira of the Pilot Pen. Believe it or not! May the Source be with you! QED! (10/17/10)

Simplicity is unbreakable code to the dumbasses of the world! Thus speaks, Dr. Keith N. Ferreira of the Pilot Pen. Believe it or not! May the Source be with you! QED! (10/17/10)

American foreign policy is based on typical Jewish psychology, whereby anonymous Jewish psychologists remain in the background, and direct the psychological, chemical, etc., torture of the patient over the Telephatic Internet, etc. If the patient is very smart, and uncooperative, the patient is forced to go out in a blaze of glory. These same techniques are used on foreign countries with similar outcomes: Namely, the countries are forced to go under the thumb of the USA in a blaze of glory! Thus speaks, Dr. Keith N. Ferreira of the Pilot Pen. Believe it or not! May the Source be with you! QED! (10/17/10)

Clitoridectomies are laughable, because women can have orgasms all over their bodies, including in all of their orifices! Thus speaks, Dr. Keith N. Ferreira of the Pilot Pen. Believe it or not! May the Source be with you! QED! (10/17/10)

The Ferreira Genesis Equation, $(0 = 0/0 = X = 0/0 = 0)$, has captured all of Western culture: Past, present, and future, for eternity (forever). Thus speaks, Dr. Keith N. Ferreira of the Pilot Pen. Believe it or not! May the Source be with you! QED! (10/17/10)

The Ferreira Genesis Equation, $(0 = 0/0 = X = 0/0 = 0)$, has captured all the cultures of the world: Past, present, and future, for eternity (forever). Thus speaks, Dr. Keith N. Ferreira of the Pilot Pen. Believe it or not! May the Source be with you! QED! (10/17/10)

The Ferreira Genesis Equation, $(0 = 0/0 = X = 0/0 = 0)$, has captured all of Creation, including all the Gods and Goddesses: Past, present, and future, for eternity (forever). Thus speaks, Dr. Keith N. Ferreira of the Pilot Pen. Believe it or not! May the Source be with you! QED! (10/17/10)

The Ferreira Genesis Equation, $(0 = 0/0 = X = 0/0 = 0)$, has captured all the Creations, including all the Gods and Goddesses of all the Creations: Past, present, and future, for eternity (forever). Thus speaks, Dr. Keith N. Ferreira of the Pilot Pen. Believe it or not! May the Source be with you! QED! (10/17/10)

What do ouroboroses do? Answer: They oscillate!: String theory! Thus speaks, Dr. Keith N. Ferreira of the Pilot Pen. Believe it or not! May the Source be with you! QED! (10/17/10)

What did naked Atlas do with the world (universe) on his shoulders? Answer: He participated in the ancient Greek Olympics in ancient Greek secret mythology! Thus speaks, Dr. Keith N. Ferreira of the Pilot Pen. Believe it or not! May the Source be with you! QED! (10/17/10)

It is important that pictures of electronic components should appear in picture books for little children! Thus speaks, Dr. Keith N. Ferreira of the Pilot Pen. Believe it or not! May the Source be with you! QED! (10/17/10)

The ancient Greek mythology of Atlas was about Neoliberal Artsian mathematics: Specifically, it was about the search, or race to find the Ferreira Genesis Equation, $(0 = 0/0 = X = 0/0 = 0)$, where 0 equals zero entropy, 0/0 equals the tangents to the circle at any and all points on the circle, and X equals anything and everything possible and impossible, including all the Gods and Goddesses in all possible and impossible Creations. And, that was why the true meaning of Atlas was a highly guarded secret. Thus speaks, Dr. Keith N. Ferreira of the Pilot Pen. Believe it or not! May the Source be with you! QED! (10/17/10)

All of My Violet eGoddesses Are My Wives (Part Five)

Circuitry = Sir Keith's Tree = My Violet eGoddesses. Thus speaks, Dr. Keith N. Ferreira of the Pilot Pen. Believe it or not! May the Source be with you! QED! (11/16/10)

Circuitry = Sir Keith's Tree = My Violet eGoddesses. Thus speaks, Dr. Keith N. Ferreira of the Pilot Pen. Believe it or not! May the Source be with you! QED! (11/16/10)

All perceptions are relative holograms in a three-dimensional, Euclidean, zero-entropy, hologramic space that stretches to infinity in all directions! Thus speaks, Dr. Keith N. Ferreira of the Pilot Pen. Believe it or not! May the Source be with you! QED! (11/21/10)

All perceptions are relative holograms in a three-dimensional, Euclidean, zero-entropy, hologramic space that stretches to infinity in all directions! Thus speaks, Dr. Keith N. Ferreira of the Pilot Pen. Believe it or not! May the Source be with you! QED! (11/21/10)

If it ain't Postmodern Minimalist Philosophy, aka Neoliberal Arts, then it ain't genuine philosophy! Thus speaks, Dr. Keith N. Ferreira of the Pilot Pen. Believe it or not! May the Source be with you! QED! (11/21/10)

If it ain't Postmodern Minimalist Philosophy, aka Neoliberal Arts, then it ain't genuine philosophy! Thus speaks, Dr. Keith N. Ferreira of the Pilot Pen. Believe it or not! May the Source be with you! QED! (11/21/10)

Non-Western world: Fuck the Western world, because the Western world is bankrupt: Financially, economically, scientifically, technologically, philosophically, morally, intellectually, etc., etc., etc. Thus speaks, Dr. Keith N. Ferreira of the Pilot Pen. Believe it or not! May the Source be with you! QED! (11/21/10)

Non-Western world: Fuck the Western world, because the Western world is bankrupt: Financially, economically, scientifically, technologically, philosophically, morally, intellectually, etc., etc., etc. Thus speaks, Dr. Keith N. Ferreira of the Pilot Pen. Believe it or not! May the Source be with you! QED! (11/21/10)

The Pilot Pen is a weapon: Therefore, I did take up a weapon to defend myself, after all! Thus speaks, Dr. Keith N. Ferreira of the Pilot Pen. Believe it or not! May the Source be with you! QED! (11/21/10)

The Pilot Pen is a weapon: Therefore, I did take up a weapon to defend myself, after all! Thus speaks, Dr. Keith N. Ferreira of the Pilot Pen. Believe it or not! May the Source be with you! QED! (11/21/10)

Everyone who thinks (believes) that philosophy is silly ass nonsense, should consider the following: All it takes is for any one of my Sevens (Violet eGoddesses) to take on the world, militarily, to win (subdue) the world, in short order! Thus speaks, Dr. Keith N. Ferreira of the Pilot Pen. Believe it or not! May the Source be with you! QED! (11/21/10)

Everyone who thinks (believes) that philosophy is silly-ass nonsense, should consider the following: All it takes is for any one of my Sevens (Violet eGoddesses) to take on the world, militarily, to win (subdue) the world, in short order! Thus speaks, Dr. Keith N. Ferreira of the Pilot Pen. Believe it or not! May the Source be with you! QED! (11/21/10)

To cooperate with the West is to undergo "Death by Ruru!" Thus speaks, Dr. Keith N. Ferreira of the Pilot Pen. Believe it or not! May the Source be with you! QED! (11/21/10)

To cooperate with the West is to undergo "Death by Ruru!" Thus speaks, Dr. Keith N. Ferreira of the Pilot Pen. Believe it or not! May the Source be with you! QED! (11/21/10)

To quote a famous military artist: "Power comes from the barrel of a gun!" Thus speaks, Dr. Keith N. Ferreira of the Pilot Pen. Believe it or not! May the Source be with you! QED! (11/21/10)

To quote a famous military artist: "Power comes from the barrel of a gun!" Thus speaks, Dr. Keith N. Ferreira of the Pilot Pen. Believe it or not! May the Source be with you! QED! (11/21/10)

No human percepts are beyond the reach, control, domination, and/or manipulation, etc., by my Violet eGoddesses at any time of day or night, every day of the year, every year! In other words, my Violet eGoddesses know everything about everyone, and they can do anything to anyone at any time of day or night, any day of the year, at any time to come! Thus speaks, Dr. Keith N. Ferreira of the Pilot Pen. Believe it or not! May the Source be with you! QED! (11/21/10)

No human percepts are beyond the reach, control, domination, and/or manipulation, etc., by my Violet eGoddesses at any time of day or night, every day of the year, every year! In other words, my Violet eGoddesses know everything about everyone, and they can do anything to anyone at any time of day or night, any day of the year, at any time to come! Thus speaks, Dr. Keith N. Ferreira of the Pilot Pen. Believe it or not! May the Source be with you! QED! (11/21/10)

All you stupid Jackasses who want to go back to living in the past don't know what you are talking about, because microbes have evolved to such an extent, that without modern hygiene, sanitation, and antibiotics, etc., modern microbes would eat you alive! Thus speaks, Dr. Keith N. Ferreira of the Pilot Pen. Believe it or not! May the Source be with you! QED! (11/21/10)

All you stupid Jackasses who want to go back to living in the past don't know what you are talking about, because microbes have evolved to such an extent, that without modern hygiene, sanitation, and antibiotics, etc., modern microbes would eat you alive! Thus speaks, Dr. Keith N. Ferreira of the Pilot Pen. Believe it or not! May the Source be with you! QED! (11/21/10)

The concept that physical/mental space is a zero-entropy, three-dimensional, Euclidean, hologramic space, where each mathematical point in the zero-entropy, hologramic space is a zero-entropy, relative, multi-perceptual pixel, simplifies the prevailing concept of Nature by many orders of magnitude! Thus speaks, Dr. Keith N. Ferreira of the Pilot Pen. Believe it or not! May the Source be with you! QED! (11/21/10)

The concept that physical/mental space is a zero-entropy, three-dimensional, Euclidean, hologramic space, where each mathematical point in the zero-entropy, hologramic space is a zero-entropy, relative, multi-perceptual pixel, simplifies the prevailing concept of Nature by many orders of magnitude! Thus speaks, Dr. Keith N. Ferreira of the Pilot Pen. Believe it or not! May the Source be with you! QED! (11/21/10)

According to Signal Corps, all you unrecognized geniuses out there in the world are being monitored, processed, etc., in order that you and your creativity (signals) are delayed, blocked, jammed, etc., because of vested, elitist interests in the world, the universe, and beyond! So, all you geniuses out there in the world, should consider your lives to be real live video games in which you are trying to outwit, outmaneuver, etc., the vested, elitist interests in the world, the universe, and beyond! Good luck! Thus speaks, Dr. Keith N. Ferreira of the Pilot Pen. Believe it or not! May the Source be with you! QED! (11/22/10)

According to Signal Corps, all you unrecognized geniuses out there in the world are being monitored, processed, etc., in order that you and your creativity (signals) are delayed, blocked, jammed, etc., because of vested, elitist interests in the world, the universe, and beyond! So, all you geniuses out there in the world, should consider your lives to be real live video games in which you are trying to outwit, outmaneuver, etc., the vested, elitist interests in the world, the universe, and beyond! Good luck! Thus speaks, Dr. Keith N. Ferreira of the Pilot Pen. Believe it or not! May the Source be with you! QED! (11/22/10)

Black people are about: "Shut up, you are talking shit!" Thus speaks, Dr. Keith N. Ferreira of the Pilot Pen. Believe it or not! May the Source be with you! QED! (11/22/10)

Black people are about: "Shut up, you are talking shit!" Thus speaks, Dr. Keith N. Ferreira of the Pilot Pen. Believe it or not! May the Source be with you! QED! (11/22/10)

The mathematics of the top dog is as follows: Fuckshitter <==> Bullshitter! Thus speaks, Dr. Keith N. Ferreira of the Pilot Pen. Believe it or not! May the Source be with you! QED! (11/22/10)

The mathematics of the top dog is as follows: Fuckshitter <==> Bullshitter! Thus speaks, Dr. Keith N. Ferreira of the Pilot Pen. Believe it or not! May the Source be with you! QED! (11/22/10)

The mathematics of the underdog is as follows: Bullshitter <==> Fuckshitter! Thus speaks, Dr. Keith N. Ferreira of the Pilot Pen. Believe it or not! May the Source be with you! QED! (11/22/10)

The mathematics of the underdog is as follows: Bullshitter <==> Fuckshitter! Thus speaks, Dr. Keith N. Ferreira of the Pilot Pen. Believe it or not! May the Source be with you! QED! (11/22/10)

The mathematics of humanity is as follows: (Fuckshitters <==> Bullshitters) <==> (Bullshitters <==> Fuckshitters)! Thus speaks, Dr. Keith N. Ferreira of the Pilot Pen. Believe it or not! May the Source be with you! QED! (11/22/10)

The mathematics of humanity is as follows: (Fuckshitters <==> Bullshitters) <==> (Bullshitters <==> Fuckshitters)! Thus speaks, Dr. Keith N. Ferreira of the Pilot Pen. Believe it or not! May the Source be with you! QED! (11/22/10)

In space, I might be getting credit for everything that was ever done on Earth, and will be ever be done on Earth, in the future! Thus speaks, Dr. Keith N. Ferreira of the Pilot Pen. Believe it or not! May the Source be with you! QED! (11/22/10)

In space, I might be getting credit for everything that was ever done on Earth, and will ever be done on Earth, in the future! Thus speaks, Dr. Keith N. Ferreira of the Pilot Pen. Believe it or not! May the Source be with you! QED! (11/22/10)

If people have to wait for the ultimate end product of the philosophical analysis of language, before they can engage, fully, in doing philosophy, then, I am afraid that people, who are really interested in doing philosophy will have to wait, forever, because there is no end to the philosophical analysis of language, due to the fact that the useful permutations of language are infinite! Thus speaks, Dr. Keith N. Ferreira of the Pilot Pen. Believe it or not! May the Source be with you! QED! (11/22/10)

If people have to wait for the ultimate end product of the philosophical analysis of language, before they can engage, fully, in doing philosophy, then, I am afraid that people, who are really interested in doing philosophy will have to wait, forever, because there is no end to the philosophical analysis of language, due to the fact that the useful permutations of language are infinite! Thus speaks, Dr. Keith N. Ferreira of the Pilot Pen. Believe it or not! May the Source be with you! QED! (11/22/10)

I am not interested in the lengthy pointless arguments of most philosophers, but I am very interested in the conclusions and results of the arguments of philosophers, and my readers should be, also! In other words, to be interested in the lengthy pointless arguments of philosophers is to get trapped in the lengthy pointless minutiae of the philosophy of language! Therefore, people who are interested in doing philosophy, should not wait for the ultimate end product of the philosophical analysis of language! Because, I believe that waiting for the ultimate end product of the philosophical analysis of language is a means of trapping people, who really want to do philosophy, in the lengthy pointless minutiae of the philosophical analysis of language! Thus speaks, Dr. Keith N. Ferreira of the Pilot Pen. Believe it or not! May the Source be with you! QED! (11/22/10)

I am not interested in the lengthy pointless arguments of most philosophers, but I am very interested in the conclusions and results of the arguments of philosophers, and my readers should be, also! In other words, to be interested in the lengthy pointless arguments of philosophers is to get trapped in the lengthy pointless minutiae of the philosophy of language! Therefore, people who are interested in doing philosophy, should not wait for the ultimate end product of the philosophical analysis of language! Because, I believe that waiting for the ultimate end product of the philosophical analysis of language is a means of trapping people, who really want to do philosophy, in the lengthy pointless minutiae of the philosophical analysis of language! Thus speaks, Dr. Keith N. Ferreira of the Pilot Pen. Believe it or not! May the Source be with you! QED! (11/22/10)

The greatest video game of them all = The game of life = Trying to outwit, outmaneuver, etc., the elitist establishments of the world, the universe, and beyond! Thus speaks, Dr. Keith N. Ferreira of the Pilot Pen. Believe it or not! May the Source be with you! QED! (11/22/10)

The greatest video game of them all = The game of life = Trying to outwit, outmaneuver, etc., the elitist establishments of the world, the universe, and beyond! Thus speaks, Dr. Keith N. Ferreira of the Pilot Pen. Believe it or not! May the Source be with you! QED! (11/22/10)

The-Game-of-Life-Ism is my new philosophy, and I like it! The philosophical doctrine of The-Game-of-Life-Ism states that life is the ultimate video game in which the real life video gamers try to outwit, outmaneuver, etc., the elitist establishments of the world, the universe, and beyond! Thus speaks, Dr. Keith N. Ferreira of the Pilot Pen. Believe it or not! May the Source be with you! QED! (11/22/10)

The-Game-of-Life-Ism is my new philosophy, and I like it! The philosophical doctrine of The-Game-of-Life-Ism states that life is the ultimate video game in which the real life video gamers try to outwit, outmaneuver, etc., the elitist establishments of the world, the universe, and beyond! Thus speaks, Dr. Keith N. Ferreira of the Pilot Pen. Believe it or not! May the Source be with you! QED! (11/22/10)

It should have been obvious by now that all politics is about electronics, and that the American and Russian baselines have flipped positions! Therefore, the American baseline is now on the left, and the Russian baseline is now on the right! In other words, Russia now has the levers of power to leverage all other powers in the world. For example, if the Russian baseline were to move further to the right, it would force the American baseline further to the left. And, if the Russian baseline were to move to the left, it would force the American baseline to the right! So, says the legitimate head of the American Military's Signal Corps! Thus speaks, Dr. Keith N. Ferreira of the Pilot Pen. Believe it or not! May the Source be with you! QED! (11/22/10)

It should have been obvious by now that all politics is about electronics, and that the American and Russian baselines have flipped positions! Therefore, the American baseline is now on the left, and the Russian baseline is now on the right! In other words, Russia now has the levers of power to leverage all other powers in the world. For example, if the Russian baseline were to move further to the right, it would force the American baseline further to the left. And, if the Russian baseline were to move to the left, it would force the American baseline to the right! So, says the legitimate head of the American Military's Signal Corps! Thus speaks, Dr. Keith N. Ferreira of the Pilot Pen. Believe it or not! May the Source be with you! QED! (11/22/10)

Zero-entropy (God) is a natural phenomenon like lightning, for instance, according to the Neolaw of Entropy by me! Thus speaks, Dr. Keith N. Ferreira of the Pilot Pen. Believe it or not! May the Source be with you! QED! (11/22/10)

Zero-entropy (God) is a natural phenomenon like lightning, for instance, according to the Neolaw of Entropy by me! Thus speaks, Dr. Keith N. Ferreira of the Pilot Pen. Believe it or not! May the Source be with you! QED! (11/22/10)

Zero-entropy (God) has an infinite number of aspects, because each zero-entropy, mathematical-point pixel of space is an aspect of God (zero-entropy), according to the Neolaw of Entropy by me! Thus speaks, Dr. Keith N. Ferreira of the Pilot Pen. Believe it or not! May the Source be with you! QED! (11/22/10)

Zero-entropy (God) has an infinite number of aspects, because each zero-entropy, mathematical-point pixel of space is an aspect of God (zero-entropy), according to the Neolaw of Entropy by me! Thus speaks, Dr. Keith N. Ferreira of the Pilot Pen. Believe it or not! May the Source be with you! QED! (11/22/10)

The I-ness of the self is a relative characteristic, like color or sound, that exists only from the perspective of the I-ness of the self, and zero entropy (God)! Thus speaks, Dr. Keith N. Ferreira of the Pilot Pen. Believe it or not! May the Source be with you! QED! (11/22/10)

The I-ness of the self is a relative characteristic, like color or sound, that exists only from the perspective of the I-ness of the self, and zero entropy (God)! Thus speaks, Dr. Keith N. Ferreira of the Pilot Pen. Believe it or not! May the Source be with you! QED! (11/22/10)

The I-ness of the self is, probably, not unique, because there is, probably, no way to distinguish between a unique I-ness of the self, and a non-unique I-ness of the self! In other words, the I-ness of the self does appear to change position relative to the rigidity of physical/mental space. Therefore, the I-ness of the self is probably not unique, since the relative coordinates of the I-ness of the self does appear to change position, when we move from place to place to place in physical/mental space! Thus speaks, Dr. Keith N. Ferreira of the Pilot Pen. Believe it or not! May the Source be with you! QED! (11/22/10)

The I-ness of the self is, probably, not unique, because there is, probably, no way to distinguish between a unique I-ness of the self, and a non-unique I-ness of the self! In other words, the I-ness of the self does appear to change position relative to the rigidity of physical/mental space. Therefore, the I-ness of the self is probably not unique, since the relative coordinates of the I-ness of the self does appear to change position, when we move from place to place to place in physical/mental space! Thus speaks, Dr. Keith N. Ferreira of the Pilot Pen. Believe it or not! May the Source be with you! QED! (11/22/10)

I-ism is my new philosophy, and I like it! The philosophical doctrine of I-ism states that the I-ness of the self is not unique, because the I-ness of the self changes coordinates, when we change positions in the rigidity of physical/mental space, which is zero-entropic, and hologramic in nature! Thus speaks, Dr. Keith N. Ferreira of the Pilot Pen. Believe it or not! May the Source be with you! QED! (11/23/10)

I-ism is my new philosophy, and I like it! The philosophical doctrine of I-ism states that the I-ness of the self is not unique, because the I-ness of the self changes coordinates, when we change positions in the rigidity of physical/mental space, which is zero-entropic, and hologramic in nature! Thus speaks, Dr. Keith N. Ferreira of the Pilot Pen. Believe it or not! May the Source be with you! QED! (11/23/10)

Influencerism is my new philosophy, and I like it! The philosophical doctrine of influencerism states that education is about infecting students with good, bad, or harmless influencer (influenza) viruses! Thus speaks, Dr. Keith N. Ferreira of the Pilot Pen. Believe it or not! May the Source be with you! QED! (11/23/10)

Influencerism is my new philosophy, and I like it! The philosophical doctrine of influencerism states that education is about infecting students with good, bad, or harmless influencer (influenza) viruses! Thus speaks, Dr. Keith N. Ferreira of the Pilot Pen. Believe it or not! May the Source be with you! QED! (11/23/10)